Bootstraps

Bootstraps:

From an American Academic of Color

Victor Villanueva, Jr.
Northern Arizona University

National Council of Teachers of English
1111 W. Kenyon Road, Urbana, Illinois 61801-1096

Project Editor: William Tucker

Interior Design: Tom Kovacs for TGK Design

Cover Design: Doug Burnett

NCTE Stock Number 03774-3050

Library of Congress Cataloging-in-Publication Data

Villanueva, Victor, 1948–
    Bootstraps : from an American academic of color / Victor Villanueva, Jr.
        p. cm.
    Includes bibliographical references
    ISBN 0-8141-0377-4 : $16.95
    1. Villanueva, Victor, 1948– 2. English language—Study and teaching—United States. 3. Hispanic American college teachers—Biography. 4. English teachers—United States—Biography.
I. Title.
PE64.V55A3 1993
420'.71'173—dc20
    [B]   93-31889
                                                              CIP

Contents

Good Debts: Words of Indebtedness

I think of how it would be if the numbers of academics of color actually reflected the demographics of the country.

Once a year I meet with others who are of color and are involved in language teaching. I tend to be the only one who teaches rhetoric: some do English education; some bilingual education; some teach literature, ethnic and traditional; there is usually a poet or two among us. Our teaching spans all grade levels. We are brown and black and yellow and red. At those meetings, we are the guests of NCTE. But our main host is Dr. Sandra Gibbs, the director of special programs for NCTE. She has no idea what those days mean to me. I don't think I know her politics, really. But I know she has a quick ear for the latent and a quick tongue for making the latent explicit. I'm glad she's there. A special thank you.

I am glad to be among other professionals of color for those few days. In those few days, we laugh, and we swap stories which tell of our ways, ways which tell of our particular cultures, ways we have in common as people of color. And we work. And our work reflects the things we have in common with many of our fellow professionals, and our work reflects the things we see and hear and feel, aggravating things sometimes, painful things.

So it is that somewhere along the way I had thought it would be a good idea to have a collection of essays that would depict how the struggles of people of color continue *after* goals are reached, after "making it." I still think it's a good idea. Rumor about the idea reached Michael Spooner, the person in charge of publications for NCTE. He asked if I had a book in the works. Only an idea.

Meanwhile, Bryan Short, a co-worker at Northern Arizona, had read a mixed-genre piece I had written for a collection on critical theory; he had also read a more straight-academic piece I intended to submit to a journal. He preferred the mixed genre, said the writing was more effective, the message worth saying, the time right. "Write a book." He is more than well-versed in the ins and outs of the academy, scholarship to institutional politics. I trust his judgment.

Before that, Anne Ruggles Gere responded to a mixed-genre essay I had written for the *English Journal.* She said there was a book there. I didn't see how at the time. But I had long ago learned that she knew things about this business that I would never understand (though she wasn't always aware that I didn't understand them). And she knew things about my potentials that I didn't always know. She never did let me get away with anything in graduate school, wouldn't let me lie down when I grew tired of poverty, indignity, insecurity, when I knew I didn't belong and couldn't do it. Anne and Bryan and Michael are the folks immediately responsible for my pursuing this book. Thanks.

To these, I must add William Irmscher, my first boss when I was a Teaching Assistant (short for teaching-on-assistant-pay). Along with Anne, Irmscher kept me in the act when I felt like the Judy to the institution's Punch. He worked behind the curtain, my knowing of his help only through rumor: Irmscher, the Indonesian puppetmaster. Indonesian puppetmasters are believed to shape destinies.

There is Sharon Crowley. There is her company: co-worker, critic, and friend. Hers was the critical call one day, after my wife and I decided that we would leave the loneliness of the academic profession; Sharon's the call that allowed me to give academics another chance, a decision I have not yet come to regret. We're in the same business, Professor Crowley and I, rhetoric and composition, attending the same meetings, knowing some of the same people, reading the same journals and books, having similar ideas. We have fun together. And even a two-minute talk in the halls is often the seed for hours of fruitful thought. Yet she is less a mentor than my academic Papo. Papo was something of my protector on the block back in Bed-Stuy, the bad-ass that no one messed with. Sharon protects me from institutional politics, a discourse I will likely never break into.

Special others. There is Bill Grabe, who casually tosses into my box linguistic things I would want to read. And my bosses at Northern Arizona (named after furniture: chairs; Freire goes on about dehumanization), Paul Ferlazzo and Sharon and Susan Foster-Cohen. I could get on in Bed-Stuy. I'm not sure I could in the academy, the day-to-day, without these chairs. Breaking into the professional academic community is tricky business for most, I'm sure. Harder still for the person of color still weighted down by a GED, my personal psychological baggage of failure. Thanks to those who believe in me.

Since I am mixing genres even here, a mix of dedication and acknowledgment. I think it important to acknowledge those editors and publishers who accepted essays I have written in the past which

appear here in larger chunks. I've been going on about the same stuff
for some time now, so I bypass the fragments and I bypass things
written for NCTE. What remains includes a chapter in *Writing With:
New Directions in Collaborative Teaching, Learning, and Research,*
edited by Sally Reagan, Thomas Fox, and David Bleich, to be published
by State University of New York Press (1993); an article which appears
in *PRE/TEXT (1993);* and a chapter which appeared in *Politics of
Writing Instruction: Postsecondary,* edited by Richard Bullock and John
Trimbur, published by Boynton/Cook in 1990. My thanks to the
editors, especially John Trimbur, for having encouraged me to write.
Thanks to the publishers for allowing what I had written to appear in
print. Thanks, also, to the NCTE Editorial Board for taking the risk
of accepting this somewhat idiosyncratic book. And thanks to Bill
Tucker, the copy editor, for laboring ever so sensitively over my every
word.

Then again, I wouldn't have written, and wouldn't be writing now,
if Mami hadn't pushed for linguistic assimilation and if Dad hadn't
remained grateful for being an American while being audibly critical
of America. I wouldn't be writing if the local parochial school hadn't
had its doors open to the poor. I wouldn't bother if students, many of
them teachers themselves, hadn't, in various ways, let me know that I
am in the right job.

And there is Carol and the babies: the preschoolers, the schoolers,
the grown up, my babies all. My babies give my life its greatest meaning.
Perhaps my greatest struggles have been in trying to meet the institution's
demands while remaining a parent in very traditional ways, not just
leaving the raising to Carol or part-time parents-for-hire. None of it
gets done as well as I'd like, but all of it does get done. And the
semblance of balance comes in my never not being a father (which I
hope makes for paternity more than paternalism in classrooms).

From Carol I continue to learn how to think in large, global, systemic
terms, in terms of politics and political economies. She helps me put
our lives in context—a global, economic context—which saves me
from the self-fulfilling prophecy that dooms the many labelled "at risk."
Much of the final chapter to this book, the post(modern)script, is
tantamount to plagiarism.

From Carol I learn that to be critical does not have to mean to be
cynical. From Carol I know of magic, of loving. And knowing love
opens up possibilities, allows one to be utopian in the midst of all that
sometimes seems hopeless. Ché Guevara believed revolutions begin

with love. Maybe loving a country and its peoples can provide for revolutionary change—more than mere reforms: true equity. Maybe. And loving brings me full circle. *A Mami* and Dad: *que Dios te bendigan.*

Prologue

"It's nobody's business," Mami would say. But I can't just say nothing about how it is I come to know some things, come to regard some theories on literacy and writing and rhetoric as more tenable than others, and how I come to think the ways I do about racism and ethnocentricity and the class system, and why I can believe in the chances for revolutionary changes in attitudes about racism and ethnocentricity and class through language and the classroom. I can't just say nothing. But there's Mami and the Latino ways: private things should remain private. So, play out the tension.

Thoughts. The I speaking to its me.

The portorican boy (that's how they say it—portorican) looks at the experiences of the African American and says, "That's racism. They can't escape their skin. No one will let them." Mami always did carry on about his good hair—curl, but no kink—his *nariz fino,* a Roman nose, she used to say. *Blancito* on the block. Steven Figueroa looked Asian somehow. Enchi (enchilada) looked more Mexican. The others looked mulatto or black. He's the white kid among the browns and blacks of Brooklyn's Williamsburg and Bedford-Stuyvesant.

Long later, a beard, long hair. The hair is not intended as a political statement, only a response to too many years of "get a haircut" and "shave again": dress codes in school, seven years in the army. Standing by a hamburger stand in the American midwest, someone speaks to him in a decidedly foreign tongue. Turns out to be Farsi. He must look Iranian. Trying to enter the All-American Crafts Fair in the Heart of America, the man behind the ticket counter asks if he is Indian, from India. He must look Indian. Sitting in a bus in Seattle, a Japanese-looking fellow handing out fliers for a Christian radio station says, "Jesus loves you, my little Jewish friend." He must look Jewish. The white kid in Brooklyn ain't just white elsewhere. He's some sort of ethnic.

Shakespeare saw Othello as black. Othello the Moor, *el morro.* There's a U.S. army base in Puerto Rico called *El Morro. El Blancito,* the white one in Brooklyn, not white elsewhere, is more the Moor than the Puerto Rican Boricua Indian or the West African black apparently, a hint of some ancient Islamic strain. "This is my son, Fidel," says his dad. Fidel, the bearded, the white guy who would not be quite white on a Seattle bus, a Kansas City crafts fair, a suburban hamburger stand. There are other Caribbean Latinos who look like him, some famous (or infamous). He's just not typical of the stereotypical. So many subtleties to the absurdities of racism.

"Congratulations on your book," says a co-worker. The department's brag sheet had announced his receiving a contract, a book on language and rhetoric and teaching from the perspective of a person of color: *Bootstraps*. But the colleague couldn't just leave it at congratulations: "Still, I have a hard time seeing you as someone of color." My guess is that he meant that as a compliment, likely having something to do with competence. The colleague must see "color" as brown and black and not quite as able (though the incompetence is a social problem, not a genetic predisposition, no doubt). With competence, the Moorish hue goes undetected.

I didn't always see myself as a person of color. Nor did I question my competence back then, though the more the awareness of color, the greater the insecurity as I grew older. But in those early years I was *el blancito,* after all. I could see myself as poor, the working class. And there is a connection between class and color, some overlap, matters to be discussed later in this book. But "color," back then, meant shades of brown, black. It hadn't occurred to me that the Puerto Rican would somehow not be white, no matter the pigment. My father's childhood friend, Archibal—no *d*—Sydney Radcliffe, Anglo named, blue eyed, blond haired. White? Likely not: many-generationed Puerto Rican, monolingual in Spanish. If not white, a Spic. No speak English, no speak, speak, spic. Language is also race in America. Spanish is color.

Yet color didn't really strike me, not really, till college, as I attempted to move within the class system, and as more of America's cultural heritage, seen through literature and through rhetoric, became clear. W. E. B. DuBois told me of the souls of black folk and the degree to which education does not overcome racism. Faulkner introduced me to the octoroon, who for all his or her success, not being seen as black elsewhere, could not transcend a black genetic line. Of course the Puerto Rican is colored: what with *el morro,* and the West African, and Columbus's Indians; what with my grandmother, Mama Pina, looking like the stereotypical American Indian; what with my brown-skinned, curly haired sister, and my brown daughter, and my Spanish surname. Octorican.

He sees himself as essentially of the same race as the majority, and knows that sometimes they do too, and he wonders how it is that what he hears and sees and feels and never seems able to escape is racism nevertheless.

He looks at the experiences of the Mexican immigrant and says, "That's ethnocentrism; they're Mexican; they're immigrants." His Dad would tell of co-workers who would ask if he had been in the portorican army. "The American. We're American citizens from birth," he'd say. "We're citizens." His Dad would tell of Operation Bootstrap, Governor Muñoz Marin's Puerto Rican prosperity program. Corporations like Pfiezer prosper, tourism does well, the Atlantic fleet does well—while the majority of the Puerto Rican people have the honor of ranking second in the nation for poverty and for food-stamp allotment, second only to American Indians. The Indian reservations: colonies within the U.S.; Puerto Rico, a U.S. possession, a colony; both have the inordinate economic dependence of neocolonialist states. Texas and Utah and Arizona and New Mexico and Colorado: colonies once. And California. The natives are not immigrants, yet not equal to other citizens.
The colonized. "You Spanish?" "Where you from?" "What's your national origin?" "What's your ethnic heritage?" Folks are quick to tell of their German or their Irish. They search for roots. Their roots are never exposed. No one seems to see their roots. Seems like everyone sees his. He doesn't think to ask them roots questions in the way they're compelled to ask him, and he doesn't see that they ask each other as a matter of course.
A manuscript in the mail: "Would you please review this bibliography of Mexican American literature?" He enjoys the literature well enough, Galarza and Anaya and others. But he knows more of Chaucer and Milton and Yeats than of Puerto Rican writers like Piri Thomas or Tato Laviera or Nicolasa Mohr. He knows Mexicans less. He has been stereotyped again: Hispanic, a monolith, all the same—in everything; all know one another; all read the same things. He doesn't even teach literature as a matter of course, ethnic or otherwise.

I teach writing, in English; and know next to nothing about bilingual education from a professional perspective. I teach and study the Greeks and the Romans and their influence on contemporary English discourse—American discourse. I study and talk about modern rhetoricians like Kenneth Burke or Wayne Booth, postmodern French cultural critics who speak in essentially rhetorical terms, like Foucault or Derrida. I am professionally distanced from the Hispanic in many ways. Not even Paulo Freire quite qualifies as Hispanic to me, insofar as I have come to know of him through non-Hispanic channels, and insofar as his Brazilian Portuguese is more foreign to me than Greek. I've probably learned more about the histories and the political economies of Mexico and Latin America from my non-Hispanic wife.

I have never stopped trying to assimilate. And I have succeeded in all the traditional ways. Yet complete assimilation is denied—the Hispanic English professor. One can't get more culturally assimilated and still remain other. People of color carry the colony wherever we go. Internal colonialism: a political economy, an ideology, a psychology.

And so he recognizes that despite the cultural differences between Puerto Ricans and the mainstream he sees himself as essentially of the same culture as the majority—even the transmitter of the majority culture—no immigrant. And he wonders how it is that what he hears and sees and feels and never seems able to escape is ethnocentrism nevertheless.

He looks at the experiences of the African American speaker of Black English, the Spanish-speaking Mexican American, Puerto Rican, or other Latino, and says, "They lack sophisticated speaking skills in the language of the majority." Then he remembers having spoken Spanish and Black English and the Standard English required at the school, seems like always, and he wonders how it is that he got sorted outside the mainstream, relegated to a vocational high school, a high school dropout. He is racially white, despite the subtle hue, a native-born citizen and lifetime resident of the continental United States, a quick study in linguistic code switching, a Ph.D. in the language and the literary traditions of the majority, a reproducer of those traditions. And still, other. And he realizes that there is more to racism, ethnocentricity, and language than is apparent, that there are long-established systemic forces at play that maintain bigotry, systemic forces that can even make bigots of those who are appalled by bigotry. Now to try to make that realization explicitly understood. It is an aim for what follows: this book.

He has made it by the bootstraps: GED to Ph.D.—an American success story. But he knows that for most like him the bootstraps break before the boots are on, that too many have no boots. So he tries to grasp at concepts like colonialism and ideology and hegemony and the ways they are imbricated with language, tries to figure this out: this book.

So how come a GED? I'll accept some blame, sure. I remember giving up. But systemic forces had an influence, surely: matters of colonialism, old-fashioned and neo- and internal; matters of race and culture and class and their manifestations in speech.

Then how a doctorate? There are always some who get through. Some *must* get through, a matter of ideological credibility in the land of opportunity, the workings of hegemony. Yet internal colonialism remains, never quite equity.

How the doctorate? I deserve some credit, sure: maturity and motivation; the bliss of ignorance, not always recognizing the systemic; and with the naiveté, the edge in being critical, in recognizing the systemic. A contradiction. It plays out this way: I didn't know what I was getting into, but knew I was getting into something not intended for the likes of me.

There are always the contradictions. Antonio Gramsci makes much of them. So does Paulo Freire. In this case there is the contradiction of achieving the inaccessible through the combination of cultural literacy with critical literacy. They are not dichotomous, necessarily. Both are necessarily important to the American of color, the colonized, the one who is American and yet other.

Containing contradictions is difficult, sometimes crazy making—a mutual affirmation and denial. American academic of color. Fully an academic. I imagine what I would do were I among the truly wealthy: lottery fantasies. I imagine that after seeing the world I would settle down to reading and to writing, learning and teaching, likely about politics and language—academics. Yet fellow academics are foreign to me in many ways, and I think they will always be, that I will always be somehow an outlander. I am of color, now fully aware of the color, and I am of poverty (not just "from" poverty), never (not even now, economically) of the middle class, not even quite the colored middle class (who are not equal with the white middle class). So I often feel alone professionally. But I just as often feel a member of a professional community—a community that extends beyond the university that employs me, a community that includes all English-language teachers. Contradictions.

I met English-language arts teachers for the first time while I was involved with a National Writing Project site. I discovered their legitimate concerns for those students of color who studied in their classrooms in numbers far greater than those of the college classroom. I also discovered how much the teachers could not understand about being of color and of poverty, but how much they would change if

they could make real changes. I discovered teachers' desperate struggles
to understand. Teachers' struggles to understand helped to explain their
acceptance of Richard Rodriguez: the second-generation child of Mexican immigrants whose own struggles made him a popular writer at
the expense of his ties to his family and to his culture. He said this
great expense is simply the cost of becoming American. The teachers
know of this, from the stories of their own forefathers and foremothers.
But there is a difference between him and them. They assimilated. Yet,
for all his fame as an American writing in English about assimilation,
his attempts at assimilation failed. He is called upon to explain the
Latino; he has not melted into the American pot.

Classroom English teachers' struggles explain their acceptance of
Mike Rose as telling of the minority. He does tell about the person of
color. But his tellings are the observer's tellings, even if told with
passion and compassion, with academic rigor and with empathy. His
remains the story of the immigrant, of bumpy roads into the middle
class. His story is not typical of the college kid, but he was a college
kid nevertheless. The teachers' struggles explain their acceptance of E.
D. Hirsch's *Cultural Literacy,* a theory espousing good old-fashioned
assimilation, what all immigrants go through. None tells our story. Us:
those who are not immigrants but long-time citizens and residents who
never quite assimilate, even when assimilation is sought after and all
the explicitly mentioned preconditions are met. There are so few of us
outside of "our fields" (like Latino literature or bilingual education).
The scarcity explains how traditions continue, good old-fashioned
traditions which have excluded too many of us for too long or else
have alienated us from our own traditions. One story follows.

But, in the telling there won't be all that much about Monday
morning and the hundred-plus students the English language arts teacher
will face. There will be some. But my experiences at teaching are
limited: a decade, almost exclusively at the college. I wasn't even a
student in the English language arts teachers' classrooms. Yet I can tell
of my journey, and I can tell of the theories, some mine, some others',
that help to explain such journeys. The theories are important, can
provide the bases for classroom practices, can suggest why some practices
might work better than others, how some practices might work counter
to what's intended.

In what follows I will tell of systems and of anomalies, of contradictions, of how the things that happened to me were systemic, and
how I managed to slip through the cracks in the hegemonic bloc. I
will tell of hegemony. What it means. How it operates. How, maybe,
to counter it. What follows will tell of the pleasures and frustrations I

experience in working within an institution that constantly seeks change and continually impedes change, of my respect and affection for nice people who are too often unwittingly unkind to people of color. Respect and affection—and a belief that most would do better by people of color—provide the impetus for this book. What follows tells of how events and observations and speculations suggest matters for further consideration by those who would do better by those of us who are of color.

My views are grounded in experience, elaborated upon by theory, and tested in research. The theory has many sources, but at bottom there is Antonio Gramsci. Gramsci tells it best, to my mind. He appeals to my sense of what rings true based on what I've known. Of all those who prompted me to write this, Gramsci resounds the loudest. For he says in his *Cultural Writings* that

> Autobiography can be conceived "politically." One knows that one's life is similar to that of a thousand others, but through "chance" it has had opportunities that the thousand others in reality could not or did not have. By narrating it, one creates this possibility, suggests the process, indicates the opening. (132)

Perhaps in narrating, the exception can become the rule—boots for everyone, strong straps.

Another theorist who stands out for me is Paulo Freire. In his ideas of how literacy instruction should take place he writes of "problematizing the existential." My sense is that he means generalizing, theorizing, and questioning the systemic based on the personal. This is what he calls *praxis:* reflection and action through language. Praxis is what I'm attempting to do here, more than providing a self-serving story, either glorious me or woe-is-me. What I'm attempting is to provide a problematic based on sets of experience: an experience which leads to a theory, a theory that recalls an experience; reflections on speculations, speculations to polemics to reflections—all with an aim at affecting what might happen in classrooms, the sites of action.

Going from experience to theory to reflection and so on will make for a text that cannot be neatly linear. Besides, linearity does not tend to come easily to the Latino. There is a rhetorical predisposition to the Latino which reflects ancient sophistry going back to the empires of Alexander, Byzantium, Islam, Spain. I will tell of this too, a glimpse at the history of rhetoric and its links to imperialism and colonialism, and a branch of applied linguistics called contrastive rhetoric. For now, I would just have it known that the alinearity is intentional, even crafted, that there is a logic. I am never *just* emoting, never *just* displaying the free associative workings of a mind. I am presenting my "ideograph," to use a term by yet another theorist I enjoy, Fredric Jameson, presenting my own ideologically influenced dialectical processes. I hope for some enjoyment for the reader in the byways which always return to the main road. Along the way, the reader will meet one Latino's mind as it is manifest and constituted in language and discourse and rhetoric.

This is an autobiography with political, theoretical, pedagogical considerations. The story includes ethnographic research. The story includes things tried in classrooms. The story includes speculations on the differences between immigrants and minorities, the class system and language, orality and literacy, cultural and critical literacy, Freire, ideology, hegemony, how racism continues and the ways in which racism is allowed to continue despite the profession's best efforts. And in its inclusions the story suggests how we are—all of us—subject to the systemic. This is the personal made public and the public personalized, not for self-glory nor to point fingers, but to suggest how, maybe, to make the exception the rule.

I The Block

biff, baff, bing, bang;
the man in the moon
and the black sedan.
the first time the Buccaneers
let you pass;
now the Buccaneers
are gonna kick your ass.

The chant rises up to the ninth floor of the projects. On the street below there are maybe a hundred boys and men, bippin' in unison: the walk of being bad, one arm swinging, an intentional hobble: bippin'. At the head of the marchers, two men, black or portorican, patches over one eye, do-rags pirate-like over their heads. Before them, two large, white dogs on chains. This is Buccaneer turf. Bed-Stuy.

But no matter what goes on downstairs, the projects are nice. They're a step up from Bartlett Street in the Williamsburg district, the block where I had lived my first thirteen years. The projects on Lafayette are new. No graffiti. No urine. Elevators. An incinerator chute on every floor. No more up and down five flights to take out the garbage. My own room, my second since ten, the first with a door, free from layer after layer of paint. My own safe window, a window that opens smoothly—and not onto the fire escape. And the bathroom: the toilet tank connected to the seat, a handle instead of a chain. The tub connected to the floor; no dead rats. A built-in shower. A wash basin. Nice. And Mami had landed a job at the New York Stock Exchange as a keypunch operator, up from saleslady, up from assembly-line worker for Standard Toycraft. And Dad had gotten a city job: mechanic's helper with the New York Transit. Good things. "Just be home by dark."

A T-card and five cents provide bus transportation to Alexander Hamilton Vocational-Technical High School. Nine periods a day— three are more or less academic, one is lunch, one PE, four shop: mechanical drawing, foundrywork, architectural drawing, carpentry. Not one full-length novel in three years of high school.

An appreciation for literacy comes from Mr. Del Maestro. He teaches drama, though he ventures into poetry on occasion. A Robert Culp-

1

like fellow, square jawed, thin but not skinny, reading glasses halfway down his nose, thin brown hair combed straight back, large hands. He had been a makeup man in Hollywood, he says. Brings movie-making to life. And for me, he brings Julius Caesar to life, removes the mist from "Chack-es-piri," as *abuela* would say it. And for those in the room not as fascinated by Julius Caesar or Prince Hamlet or poor Willy Loman as I am, those who are—in teacher talk—disruptive, Mr. D forgoes the pink slip to the principal, meets the disrupter downstairs, in the gym, twelve-ounce gloves, the matter settled. He has a broad definition of art. He knows the world—and he understands the block, *el bloque,* what kids today call "the hood." Mr. D was as close to color as any teacher I had known in school.

Color isn't always race when it comes to teachers. It's an attitude, more an understanding of where we live than where we're from. We came from many places back on the block. A teacher would have had to go a long way to understand and convey an understanding of all those where-froms. But a teacher could have looked around and known the where-at. Few did, even among those who were racially of color.

There were two African American teachers: Mrs. Miller, the English lit teacher, and a music appreciation teacher whose name I've forgotten, except to remember it was a French name. They weren't oreos or going about "incognegro." I can't imagine anyone saying they were trying to pass. They were black. But there was also something like what Signithia Fordham calls racelessness to them. "Mr. Musique" dressed in shark-skin suits, starched white shirts with collar pins, thin ties, his hair in a process, horned-rim glasses. He played Beethoven and Mozart and Rossini in class, took us to see *West Side Story* at Radio City Music Hall; took us to see two Broadway plays. He was an interesting character. He cared. But he was far from the block now. "Artsy fartsy," we'd say, not one of us, not like Mr. D, who never pretended to talk in Black English or even to assert that he understood the ghetto. Mr. Musique cared, but remained aloof somehow.

Mrs. Miller was straight, not tough and funny like Mrs. Roach, Irving's mom, or like Mrs. Washington, Butch's mom, or the other moms that hung out on the stoop in summer:

> Hey, you. You! Little Spanish boy. You better *get* out of that street
> when there's a car comin', or your momma gonna come down
> and whoop the rice and beans right outa you.

No such talk from Mrs. Miller. She would address us as Mr. Scriva and Mr. Jackson and Mr. Villa-nu-eva. We could appreciate the respect. But there could have been respect *and* some acknowledgment of our ways of having to live in Bed-Stuy. Not one of us could imagine her saying "Spanish boy" or "pretty little nigger." We talked about it. She was not of the block.

And the distances were even greater between students and many of the rest of the teachers. Spanish was taught by Mr. Hauser (trying to teach Spanish to thirty bilingual kids). We didn't know about dialects, prestige, and the like, just about right and wrong. He was wrong. Shop was taught by Mr. "LaVek." He spelled it l-e-v-e-s-q-u-e. We didn't get it. But he was all right, except for calling us "you people": "You people need to learn a trade." Didn't seem to us that he had gotten around needing a trade, even if he was now a teacher.

It had always been, and would always be, that way. In grade school, the nuns. The Sisters Mary Discipline at the parochial school that charged only a dollar a month tuition. All white. Many years later, college: an East Indian teaches an English course, a Vietnamese teaches French, a German (I think) teaches British lit. Not typical, perhaps, but not colored or minorities, to my thinking (more on this later). The rest: all white. And not one of them willing to acknowledge our social conditions.

But back then, for one semester in a vocational high school in Brooklyn, there was one. Mr. D could speak *with* us. To speak of Julius Caesar was to speak of how fighting, ganging up, was seen as a solution for many people over a long time. But the power really depended on knowing how to use language, the language of Mark Antony, for instance. Mr. D provided the spark that would flare again some thirteen years later.

He wondered where they all came from, these men, mostly men in an all-boys school, men with their smooth, puffy cheeks, round bellies, rumpled suits, and wrinkled shirts. And why they were here. Some cared, he could tell: the wiry French Canadian who taught foundry, the crazy Jewish "professor" who insisted on the title, the neat little TV-sitcom kind of a white guy in the starched lab coat. Interested, though not knowing, and not seeming to want to know. But mostly, they seemed disinterested, detached, these imparters of wisdom who didn't even seem to know where they were working. Their ignorance affected their credibility.

Didn't seem to be a day go by when there wasn't a fight in the halls at Hamilton. A redhead on his back; a portorican kneeling on Red's shoulders, portorican fists pounding a red head to the floor, blood, smeared brown on Red's face, smeared red on the portorican's black fist. So commonplace that no one even stops to look. A bored apple-on-a-stick in an overworn suit picks up the portorican by the collar, tells him to get to his next class, gives Red a hand up, tells him to go to the lavatory to clean himself. Then the apple walks away. Minimal maintenance. Why doesn't he take his education and *do* something with it?

Mr. D was different: talking about working on Marlon Brando's nose for *Viva Zapata* and how roads not taken can still be gotten to in later life after reading Frost, and making hairs stand on end when reading Mark Antony's funeral speech. And telling us how to stand, left foot outside, how to put the whole body behind a punch, in the midst of what was supposed to be a disciplining.

This was Papi's world: the Buccaneers and the Mao Maos, gang wars in the streets and in the halls of Hamilton, teachers talking in tired monotones, foundry and carpentry and drafting. He'd rather read. But this was the world. And there would be no college.

There would be no college, and he couldn't carry a tune, wasn't much interested in learning a musical instrument, wasn't a graceful dancer. The entertainment industry was out. At baseball, teams would argue about which team he'd be on: "No, men (pronounced with a shortened *n*), *you* take him." Baseball was out. He joined the Police Athletic League, behind his folks' back, to learn boxing. Music, baseball, and boxing: that's how portoricans got money legally. Never told his folks about the boxing (still hasn't). They would not have approved. First time in the ring, sixteen-ounce glove to the bridge of the nose, a white flash, a sick feeling in the stomach, tears. Boxing would be strictly a spectator sport after that. But it was good to know he could handle himself in the halls of Hamilton. No running in the halls.

One day he boarded the train headed toward Jamaica in Long Island, to a Weider outlet to buy the basic 110-pound weight set. He was scared to be round bellied and thin armed in this new block, in Hamilton. Got the set, carried it on the train, back to his Bed-Stuy bedroom. Papo (Manny Galindez, a neighborhood tough, later a Vietnam victim, Papi's friend) would be his training partner. Between Papo and *Muscle Builder* magazine, Papi got fit enough not to look like those who permanently carry invisible but easily discernible kick-me signs. He could look the bad-asses in the eye, his shoulders back, left hand swinging slightly behind the body, right hand pulling up his pants pocket, an exaggerated hobble. He be bippin'. Less brave than bravado. He could talk shit on the block when a confrontation seemed eminent: glasses off, fists loosely clenched, one poised near the hip, the other higher, over the solar plexus, eye-to-eye: "Lessee how bad you are." Only came to blows once in all the time in Bed-Stuy and Hamilton and later in Compton, near Watts. Papo, Manny, would wonder aloud how Papi could "talk-the-talk and walk-the-walk" and still be "so white" in private and do so well in school.

Later, California. East Compton. Same old ghetto—but even more of the motions, since no one thought in terms of college, yet no one was taught a trade. Just do time. School becomes more a preparation for prison than for industry: doin' time. Transfer to Dominguez. He is foreign: not white, not black, not Mexican. And since no college, where the white boys with their cars and motorcycles were headed, and since no trade, he'd get a job, stop doin' time. Drop out.

He knew about getting money—how-ever (colloquial for "by whatever means")—and *filling* time instead of *doing* it.

When he was a kid (anyone not a teenager, according to teenagers). Saturdays he'd collect pop bottles and trade them in for the deposits, or go to the local A&P and offer to help old women with their groceries. Sometimes they would give him candy or fruit in return for the help. He'd be courteous. Return to the A&P. Try again. More often the bottles and the grocery service would provide enough money for the movies. For a while, he had tried his hand at shining shoes on Graham Avenue, across from the A&P, across from the Alba, the Spanish movie house that showed English movies and five cartoons and three Three Stooges or a cliff-hanger on Saturdays for twenty-five cents. And, if he was lucky, he could hide under the seats in the balcony and stick around to see the Spanish horror movies. But when it came to shining shoes, he'd make a quarter here and there from the PR pimp in the Jew Canoe—a fancy Cadillac car—the pimp giving some business to the little PR hustler. But the shoe-shine boy just trying to get to the movies couldn't compete with the old colored guy who made music with the brushes and with the popping of buff cloths; couldn't compete with the old man's fire show as he lit the can of wax to bring oils to the surface, a spit shine in nothing flat, no wax on the socks, one dollar and always a tip. There was more money in collecting bottles and "Help you with your groceries, Ma'am?"

Sometimes there was more money in a straightened-out hanger and some really well-worked wet gum to fish out quarters from the sewers. He got a half-dollar once that way and a truly perfect glassy. He was a marbles hustler. He tried pitching pennies for movie money, but just couldn't beat Hershel Jacobs, his friend the Jewrican, Jewish father, Spanish mother. Hershey put an English on his pennies that caused them to roll up on edge and lean against the wall.

All he needed was admissions money. He always managed a bag of popcorn or a box of Goobers or, sometimes, maybe even bon-bons, in return for reading the credits and whatever else showed up on the screen in writing (the letter in her hand, the newspaper headline that would spin to a stop covering the screen, subtitles when the bad guys spoke German or Japanese). It wasn't a matter of bargaining; it was just what happened: "*Mira,* men, get some shit for the professor. *¿Que quierez, blancito?*"

And if the money had been good that week, or if there had been enough money at home to give him fifty cents for taking down the garbage and dusting the furniture, he would venture to Manhattan: new movies on 42nd Street, sixty-five cents, a new movie and a live stage show at Radio City Music Hall, one dollar, chandeliers and red carpets, vendors in uniform, the banner that read "Cooled by Refrigeration." But going uptown meant no one to buy snacks. No money to waste on buying tokens for the train. Climb to the canopy that covered the stairs to the el, hang, swing onto the platform. Or wait for the train, jump the turnstile, and get on the train before the cashier guy got out of the cage. The boy wasn't much of a scrapper, but he could jump and climb fences faster than anyone, even over barbed wire, usually without a nick. Pointed shoes: "Portorican fence climbers," the guy at Thom McCann called them. He'd need those shoes when he decided to walk to Manhattan, going through the Italian neighborhood on this side of the Brooklyn bridge, the Micks on that side. Things would feel safer by 14th Street: the college kids, white kids with baggy, frumpy pants, and equally baggy and frumpy shirts, sandals, and no socks. He wondered why they didn't wear shoes when they could afford them.

When there was no money, he would walk to Fulton Street, past Pratt Institute in Bed-Stuy. He'd walk past Fort Greene Park: "Hey, kid, got a nickel? Let me check your pockets, and I keep what I find." Thank Thom McCann for Portorican fence climbers. His destination: the Brooklyn public library's air-conditioned reading room: cool, plush chairs, Courier and Ives prints of snow and sleighs on the walls. He'd spend the day. He read *Dracula* one day, *Frankenstein* another. He'd read them again in college: The Nineteenth Century and the Literature of Decadence.

He'd heard a song once, "Camp Grenada." A line in the song went something like

And the Head Coach wants no sissies
So he reads to us from something called *Ulysses.*

There's laughter in the record. So, curious, he found two books with that title. One was incomprehensible. It was probably the one by James Joyce, he thinks now. He read the other one. By Homer. And Thor in Marvel Comics took on new meaning. And suddenly there was more to the Hercules movies than Steve Reeves and buxom Italian women.

By the third grade I had found my niche: grammar and spelling. Reading had little to do with school. School reading was the catechism, Dick and Jane, and poetry that made me think of bubbling brooks and babbling idiots. I don't remember science much: Galileo dropping something from the leaning tower at Pisa and Newton seeing it fall in England somewhere. One had to do with the speed of gravity, and the other the law of gravity, I realize now. I wrote a paper about John Herschel Glenn, Jr., though, in the eighth grade, his defying gravity in orbiting the planet. So much for Newton and Galileo. I was good at math. Professor Steinberg in the ninth grade told my parents I should be a mathematician. He liked the paper I had written on "Euclid, the Father of Geometry." I was good at math, but better at that paper. Writing it meant a day at the New York Public Library in Manhattan, the big one, the one with the lions in front. Math was a challenge, but not a pleasure. Parsing sentences, diagramming, now that was fun.

Language was—is—my joy. Spelling was easy: just repeat three times, make up a sentence, and the word was stuck in the brain. And the tricky ones had fun rhymes:

> *i* before *e*
> except after *c*
> or when sounded like *a*
> as in *neighbor* and *weigh.*

Religion provided the fun in language, its slip and slide. I was later delighted to see that Kenneth Burke, a twentieth-century rhetorician, used religious terms to explain the nature of language as symbolic. The ultimate achievement of rhetoric, he writes, would be consubstantiation. I knew that word. The fourth grade. *Consubstantiation*, a hefty word, more impressive than m-i-ss-i-ss-i-pp-i, but what did it mean? That the Father, the Son, and the Holy Ghost were three beings in one. Later I would find that Mohammed rose to prominence because of two hundred years of trying to work out an idea like the Trinity. But then, when I puzzled aloud about the Trinity, Sister Georgette would say, "It's a mystery." I loved mysteries, had read all of the Hardy Boys and all of Sherlock Holmes. And mysteries had logical solutions. Sister Georgette said this mystery would be cleared up in the next life (given some preconditions in this one). *Consubstantiation* never got nailed down.

There was no precision to the language of religion. And even as I puzzled and questioned and even got annoyed, I enjoyed the imprecision.

But it was a secret, private pleasure. Language was supposed to be precise: "don't split infinitives," "use the plural in the subjunctive," "don't use double negatives." At home I would correct my folks when an English rule was broken. Yet, even as I was dogmatic and doctrinaire at home, I understood there were different rules on the block. On the block, not only could infinitives be split, but if emphasis was desired, words could be split (fanfuckentastic); the subjunctive would be solidified into a state of being (if I be you); and, like other languages which don't make some silly analogy between language and mathematics, more negatives simply meant greater emphasis. "Ain't no way" never implied there was a way. And "Ain't nobody tellin' me nothin' about nothin'" never implied that the speaker was open to suggestion. Add a *mira* on one end and a *men* on the other, and you got portorican Black English: "*Mira,* ain't no way nobody tellin' me nothin' about nothin', men." Mom would forbid such talk at home: no "cool" no "dig" no "men." Gang talk. The dogma found reinforcement from Mami.

Spanglish was simply Spanish: "Papi, *dame la* hammer." No need to correct; that wasn't English. Spanish and Spanglish at home. Standard English at home and in school. Black English on the block. Different rules in different places. I knew that. Language was not the problem of the would-be dropout.

I was taken aback when I learned of Black English in college, that William Labov and his researchers had to come to the block to talk with African American and Puerto Rican kids, discovering that the English we spoke was consistent, was rule-governed. I wasn't shocked at his discovery, but shocked that the brightest of the bright, Ph.D.'s, college professors and scientists, would know so little about the block, could banter in foreign tongues like French and German and know so little about America's Englishes. And I was all the more shocked to discover what Labov was countering.

The graduate student attends his very first professional conference, New York, 1984, the Conference on College Composition and Communication. He will be the respondent and recorder in a panel with Anne Ruggles Gere, Sarah Warshauer Freedman, Anne Matsuhashi, Melanie Sperling—big names, he later discovers. Attendance at the panel session is good, but hardly the expected numbers. Everyone, it seems, is attending a session featuring Marlene Scardamalia, representing Bereiter and Scardamalia. One of the "names" at his panel session whispers that she wishes she could attend Scardamalia's talk. Bereiter and Scardamalia had developed a sophisticated theory based on sophisticated research on the cognitive processes involved in writing, complete with sophisticated flowcharts depicting long-term memory, short-term memory, and the like. He was dumbfounded. Did scholarship reside in short-term memory? Wasn't this the same Carl Bereiter who had developed the verbal-deprivation theory, that African American children's school problems were linked to their poor language abilities? Wasn't this the same Carl Bereiter who had prompted Labov to study language in the inner city?

I'm somewhat less incensed today, if it's possible to be "a little incensed." I can be gracious, say that Bereiter and Scardamalia's work provides a suggestive tool with which to study writing processes. Applied linguistic study in discourse analysis finds Bereiter and Scardamalia helpful (Grabe and Kaplan). And there does seem to be a move toward integrating studies that appear to look solely at the cognitive with those that appear to be concerned with the social (e.g., Flower). I now know of *ad hominem* arguments, know it's not right to condemn the work by condemning the man, or even his past work. But there is the past work. And discussion of orality and literacy and cognitive capability which recalls that past work is still with us. I can still be upset that there doesn't seem to be a looking back at the harm done, the harm that reemerges, no apologies, no explanations, seems like no memory.

In a 1972 article in the *Atlantic Monthly,* William Labov described the work of Carl Bereiter. As Labov tells it, Bereiter and his associates were hoping to provide an alternative to genetic explanations for African American children's poor performance in schools. What they came up with was an environmental explanation. The problem was that the environment they focused on was not the school, not where the races and the cultures collide, but the African Americans' home environments. The theoretical jumping-off point was a misapplication of the work of British sociologist Basil Bernstein. Although I'll have more to say on Bernstein later, here it would be enough to say that Bernstein saw that home environments reinforced particular speech patterns, and that the speech patterns of home reinforced social class stratification. That is, Bernstein believed that the middle class and the working class utilized certain speech codes. And since schools are most representative of the middle class, the language of working-class kids placed the working-class students at a disadvantage in school. Bernstein's earlier work was fraught with problems, among them a rather obvious middle-class bias—that the middle-class and its language are superior. But the biggest problem with Bernstein was how he got interpreted in the United States.

In the United States, the argument went, class delineations are not as clearly marked as they are in England, the pervasive myth of America as the classless society. Bernstein's initial research, for example, compared students enrolled in a grammar school (what we would consider college prep), with kids in a vocational school. "No such thing in America." A funny argument, given that I attended one in Brooklyn, which is still technically in America. Since there was no such thing in America (Labov said that this was a matter of "Academic Ignorance"), "class" became interpreted as "color." There are overlaps, but there are also differences.

So Bereiter and his crew (and other researchers as well, for instance, Cayer and Sacks) studied the speech of African American children. Bereiter studied four-year-olds from Urbana, Illinois (not exactly Bed-Stuy or Harlem or Chicago's Southside or Watts). Four-year-old African American children are taken to see the Professor and his crew at the University. The white, male professor says,

"Who do these things belong to?"

And the child says,

"They mine."

"What do you have there?"

"Me got juice."

"Look!" pointing to a picture. "Where's the squirrel?"

"In the tree."

I made up the questions, but the responses are the ones Labov quotes as having been supplied by Bereiter and by Siegfried Englemann as the children's words. And the conclusion that the researchers came to was that these children elicited the "language of [the] culturally deprived . . . not merely an underdeveloped version of standard English, but . . . basically [a] non-logical mode of expressive behavior" (60). The upshot for the researchers was to treat the children "as if they had no language at all" (60). The theory of cultural deficiency which followed was the "verbal-deprivation theory." Here's how Labov sums up Bereiter's theory:

> [B]lack children from the ghetto area are said to receive little verbal stimulation, to hear very little well-formed language, and as a result are impoverished in their means of verbal expression. It is said that they cannot speak complete sentences, do not know the names of common objects, cannot form concepts or convey logical thoughts. (59)

Labov counters. The answer about the squirrel is hardly a reflection of illogic. Almost anyone, whatever her race or social-class standing, could have given the same response, word-for-word. The *Me got juice* is not likely intended to mean *The juice got me*, which would then be truly illogical; all that's involved is confusion concerning when to use the objective and when to use the nominative—a confusion not unusual among young children, black and white. And *they mine* is not a reflection of poor logic because of a lack of understanding of the logical relationship implicit in the use of the copula (verbs of "to be"); *they mine* only reflects a contraction rule, which is to delete single consonants representing *is*, *have*, or *will*. Labov gives the linguist's response.

Labov goes with his own crew, which includes African American researchers from Harlem, to Harlem itself. The researchers begin by breaking down authority structures: sitting at eye level with the interviewees, using street language, discussing subjects of interest to the interviewees. Labov finds that the ghetto kids, rather than being non-logical, enjoy playing logic games, holding and winning arguments for the sake of winning. So, rather than seeing them as verbally deprived, Labov establishes that the ghetto kids receive a great deal of verbal stimulation, even if in a dialect foreign to the white, middle-class researchers.

Arthur Jensen reacts. He says something like "See, the environmental explanation doesn't hold up. More likely, blacks are genetically incapable of 'cognitive conceptual learning,' Level II intelligence. The best they can do is Level I, 'associative learning.' "

Then Thomas Farrell—a decade later. He says something like "Wait a minute. I can't accept this genetic explanation. And it *is* clear that 'black ghetto youths' are very vocal. In fact, that's the problem: they reside in an oral culture. Look at the games they play—word games. But look at how they miss out on sophisticated, embedded thinking. I mean, look at their syntax. It's narrative, one clause attached to another instead of subordinated. And look at the copula: Black English lacks a full realization of 'to be.' Just like preliterate black Africans, American blacks can't reach Level III or Level IV of cognitive development." This isn't a quote. But it is what he says in "IQ and Standard English."

'Round and 'round she goes. Since the question is always "what's wrong with them," the answer gets repeated too: bad language equals insufficient cognitive development.

Academic ignorance. There is the ignorance, for instance, in not considering that Piaget, whose development scale seems to be the measure (those "levels"), was a biologist by training, explicitly concerned with the biological and the logical-mathematical (Rose, "Narrowing the Mind" 281, 283). Piaget's most noted works were not concerned with culturally relativistic notions of cognition, as are, say, psychologists Scribner and Cole's work among multiliterate Liberians (who are literate in English, Arabic, and an indigenous script, Vai). Scribner and Cole found that different cognitive abilities reflect different social needs. Anthropologist Shirley Brice Heath goes so far as to say that the whole oral-literate dichotomy is spurious in America, that there isn't a continuum where we can say "mainly oral" or "mainly literate"; rather there are shifting oral and literate tendencies (*Ways With Words*, "Protean Shapes"; see also Rose, "Narrowing the Mind"). There is ignorance in not recognizing that Piaget himself lightened up later, adjusting the ages at which American children would arrive at the stage of formal operations. The stage of formal operations is occurring in later adolescence among American children, the age group of most of our college freshmen (Bergstrom).

But perhaps the most ethnocentric notion concerns the copulative. It is *more* complex within Black English, not less, than it is in Standard English. "I *been* gettin' the hammer" says that the effort has been taking place for some time and is still being undertaken. Look at how much effort is involved in a dialect-translation. It also strikes me that if the copulative verb is the measure of abstract intelligence, America has spent the last half-century competing with (and sometimes losing to) a people whose language has no copulative. Are we to say that Russians are stuck in Level I, not to mention the many other peoples of the globe whose languages have no copulative? Sometimes it seems that it's the American academics who have a literacy problem.

Perhaps such signs of academic ignorance can be blamed on a system that pushes academics to publish prematurely. Perhaps we can blame a system that promotes tight specialization and does not allow for ranging beyond a specific field. I'll have a few words to say about such things later. But limitations imposed on academics notwithstanding, there remains the problem that the public at large and those who go to the professors to learn, to become teachers, and the professors themselves, put a lot of stock on Ph.D.s and research tables and the printed word. The result is that too many accept the answers, including those who are the victims of the problems and the victims of the solutions. A critical perspective requires a historical perspective. We can forgive, but we should not forget.

Mom thought he hadn't been accepted by the local college-prep high school because of a kind of political economy, because the family had not contributed to the Bishop's Fund, made a pledge to donate a percentage of the family income. Mami loves him, he knows. She's trying to find explanations for what happened. But he knows, the tests told him—he isn't as smart as Mom thinks he is.

He still suffers that fear today, thirty years later, Ph.D., publications, and all. He knows the politically liberal academic. He has seen the liberal's fear of being honest with people of color about their abilities; the fear of being considered a bigot or the fear that the person of color would be permanently hurt for something not of the person of color's own doing, the disadvantages seemingly inherent in our society. He holds on to the fear because he has seen the forced acceptance of people of color purely on the basis of color. He has seen that tokenism, even when well-motivated, even though somehow necessary, makes things seem equitable when they aren't equitable at all, so that the same handful rises quickly to positions of prominence. He sees sense in Affirmative Action. He is sometimes grateful. He is often leery. He's the only portorican rhetorician he knows. In terms of others of color, the action isn't affirmative enough. In terms of his being one acted upon affirmatively, he always wonders if, maybe, he isn't as smart as people say he is.

The summer of 1962. Mom and Dad and his month-old sister (*la trigueña,* coffee brown, a portorican color, not the Mexican's brown, not the African American's brown). A week or two ago they had sat in the third-row pew of All Saints, watched with pride as he walked up the altar steps in his cap and gown to receive special recognition for spelling and for penmanship, pride as they heard him receive honorable mention in mathematics. Now he stands on the sidewalk alongside the projects on Lafayette Avenue, wondering what he is going to do with his life. Without St. Patrick's there would be no being a doctor; there would be no Howard University, the only university anyone talked about, even though NYU and Columbia were just across the bridge. And then what? Not the factories; not a keypunch operator. It was the day that he figured out that doing well in school hadn't paid off. It was the day that Dad became smarter, not to be dismissed as easily as Mom would dismiss his own political pessimism, not to be dismissed as easily as he, himself, had dismissed Dad, what with the sisters saying much of what Mom said. Dad would just say, from time to time, "*Cuidao, Papi.* They try to keep us stupid." Summer of '62 was his *Easter 1916*. From Yeats:

He, too, has resigned his part
In the casual comedy;
He, too, has been changed in his turn,
Transformed utterly:
A terrible beauty is born.

II An American of Color

A party, a bloody knife hanging from a hanging arm, eye level, Mom and Dad by the hand, running. Maybe three years old. Brooklyn. The picture remains, forty years later.

Seated behind a pegboard desk in the middle of a furnitureless living room, 41 Bartlett Street, Williamsburg, Brooklyn, Mrs. Ashell nearby, Dad walking in with a roll of linoleum. Why this memory? Maybe a three-year-old's sense of affluence: a step up from the storefront flat.

Walking from Bartlett to John Lee's hand laundry, alone. Maybe aged four. From Bartlett to somewhere near the Myrtle Avenue el. Shortest person on street corners. The only one waiting for lights to turn green. No memory of anyone asking where his Mommy is.

Just last week, 1992, Flagstaff, Arizona. A little three- or four-year-old child is wandering around the supermarket. A concerned woman bends over: "Did you lose your Mommy?" The same week, the same store, a little three- or four-year-old American Indian child is wandering, bawling loudly. People stop and stare. No one asks.

Sometime around six, the television. All kinds of kids, some of them strangers, congregate in the living room on Sunday evening for Walt Disney. The rest of the week, there are the Uncles who emcee cartoon shows, and there is Buffalo Bob, Lucy, Ralph Cramden. It was nice to see someone who lived like we did, maybe a little worse: loudmouth Ralph and his "one a dese days, Alice." He talked like the Micks, the Patties, the policemen. Some part of me has always been thankful that Ricky Ricardo was Cuban, even if he did sound portorican, what with his exaggerated accent, his complacency at the jibes on his accent. I stopped watching when Lucy and Ricky moved from the block to the 'burbs. I didn't need Ricky. I had Zorro. On Wednesday nights I could stay up past bedtime to watch Zorro. He was my special hero. On TV, he alone gave the Latino dignity for me. The Cisco Kid and Pancho were too foreign—another time, another place, another Spanish. Pancho was sillier than Ricky. But there was something Latino and not Mexican about Zorro, Don Diego, Don Alejandro—something old-world, Spaniard. Mami called my grandfather Don Basilio. Mami, especially, liked to claim Spain. I don't think I understood the colonial picture being presented in Zorro, just knew that the Latino could have a dashing, good-looking Robin Hood too.

Time and place and television didn't quite come together in the child's mind. I thought Beaver lived in another time, closer to the present than the Lone Ranger, even closer than Sky King, but not the present, not the 1950s I knew. It hadn't occurred to me that there would be Beavers in other places, neighbors on a global scale. The Cleavers, Sky King and Penny, the Lone Ranger and Tonto (Mami: "*Mira, tonto!*" when I would do something dumb; "Wake up, dummy," same thing). Not one of those TV folks fit my idea of contemporary Americans.

Before we got the neighborhood TV, before lessons on Liberty Statues and melting pots in school, the Americans I knew were the older folks who cared for me: portoricans from the family, Enchi's mom, *la comai,* portorican for *comadre,* godmother; and from as far back as I can remember, there was the old Jewish woman and the old Chinese man.

It wasn't a *barrio,* really, Williamsburg, Brooklyn, where I grew up before we moved up to Bed-Stuy. There was no one overriding ghetto culture, "ghetto" in the formal sense, an ethnic way-station to assimilation. We were portoricans, mostly, but not all alike: some of us *nuyorcinos,* natives to New York, Spanglish speakers: *"Dame la cuada"*; "Give me the quarter"; some of us from great cities on "the Island," like San Juan and Rio Piedras, pronouncing my name *"Vi-lya-nueva"*; some of us *jibaros,* country folk, with their strange Spanish: *"Bi-ja-nueba."* We were browns. We were black, the African Americans of the block, almost exclusively, it seemed, pouring out of one house on Bartlett Street, my street, the block. And we were many other colors, the world's poor. There was a *barrio* in Manhattan, Spanish Harlem, where *mi Tia Fela* lived, where there were more PRs hanging out on front stoops, and fewer broes, fewer of *los negros* who were not portorican, where there were more Cochifrito signs. So, it wasn't a *barrio,* but Bartlett Street and the Williamsburg district were the block.

The block had many hues and many sounds, mainly black and brown hues and sounds, but others as well, yellows and olives, and variations on white. Except for the Whites I would meet later, except for the middle class (having met the truly wealthy where my *abuela* lived as a resident cook for a Central Park family), I grew up among the poor, some passing through, some permanent residents.

Mrs. Ashell was never not an old woman: wrinkled face with wire-rimmed glasses, white hair in a topknot, print housedresses that buttoned up the front, nun's shoes. She lived next door, the next apartment. Yet her home was older. Always dark. It even smelled of old. Milk bottles on the fire escape, an ice box, not a refrigerator. Mrs. Ashell would speak of the old country, of being a greenhorn, when Sol was a doughboy, the change in the neighborhood when the *schwartzes* moved in, her Sonny wanting to put her away (probably to a retirement community, Sonny, the successful lawyer). From Mrs. Ashell came the smell of potato pancakes, latkes, an offering on Sunday mornings, knishes on occasion, matzah balls and chicken fat (pronounced something like *fiat*) when I was sick, with a *gesundheit* or a "Bless you" but no "God bless you." From her I knew of *yalmalkes* and *sheitelah*. And I was *bubbela*, sometimes *bubby*.

Mrs. Ashell. She had likely lived in that third-floor apartment next to ours longer than my folks had been alive. And I knew that, what with the icebox and all. She was America, but she was not as American as my family and me. Mom and Dad would talk of life *en la isla*. *La isla* was part of America. The old country was not.

A tale from "the Island."

Story has it that my mother had been sold into servitude to a wealthy Chicago family. She had been shipped to Chicago to save her from my father, if I remember rightly. Dad, fresh out of the army, followed her there, and together they fled to New York. That was in 1947. I was born a year later. Their telling was not political; it was romantic. There was no "Can you imagine!?" My guess was that it was easily imaginable on the Island. I get the sense that they even felt they had committed a wrong in not having abided by the contract that had conscripted my mother. Their telling is of a love story. And it is. A forty-four year marriage, as I write this, no trial separations.

So it was that I remember thinking that Mom was so American that she could be bought and sold; Dad so American that he could come and go. Mrs. Ashell had to have papers, a stay at Ellis Island, no talk of having gone back to the Jewish ghetto of London. She was foreign. I was American.

John Lee owned a Chinese hand laundry. I would go to his place during lunch or after school. I think of John Lee whenever I see Edward G. Robinson in *Key Largo*. Few parallels in the personalities, likely. But there was something in the way John Lee and Edward G. Robinson wore their fifties, broad, pleated pants, the waist high over round bellies, so high that their torsos seemed short, still shorter by broad ties; something in the way each held a cigar. Just that John Lee had the eyes of an Asian, but then, so did Edward G. Robinson. Stereotypes can be a bother.

Maybe age eight, I asked John Lee (who was never John or Mr. Lee) his age. "Sickty-fye Chinee; sickty-foe Amelican." Thick black hair, endless energy, laughing loudly when he would take me on amusement park rides in Coney Island: he didn't seem sixty-four or sixty-five to me. Mami explained that the Chinese counted life from inception. No conflict. That was their way, and it made sense. We had our way, and it made sense too.

That there are different worldviews, different notions of what constitutes reality, was always a given. That this is a heavy philosophical concern among academics today, even a radical rhetorical concern, only shows the limits of experience within a stratified society. Freire writes about "experts on Marx" who have never had a cup of coffee in a worker's home. How much can they know, really?

John Lee had a wife in Kowloon. He had supported her for years, thirty-five years or thereabouts. John Lee owned a high-rise apartment building in Kowloon, too. I have no idea what his wife looked like. There was a framed picture of his apartment building in the "almost-a-back room" of his laundry though.

The almost-a-back room was the social center. It was where we went when the laundry was closed. The kitchen was there, a table and chairs, a vinyl couch, the bathroom. The front room held a narrow entrance for customers, a counter with chicken wire to the ceiling, a small two-foot by two-foot opening with a little door where tickets and money and bundles of clothes wrapped in butcher paper would pass. I'd help wrap, sometimes count out change. On the other side of the counter were two large ironing tables, maybe six-feet square, with heavy irons, small tubs where the irons would be dipped before hitting a shirt, steam spewing out; beside the irons, copper bottles with what looked like kazoos attached for blowing mist over stubborn wrinkles, a tabletop steam roller, where starched collars and cuffs got pressed, a picture on the wall of Chiang Kai-Shek in full military regalia. Between the front and the back, "walls" of painted wood sheets on studs and a curtain, making four walls that surrounded a bed and a dresser. It always smelled of incense in that little area, the bed's room, not much larger than the bed. I would sleep there when I was still young enough to require naps.

The "real back room" held a coal-burning potbelly stove in the middle, four large tubs and a large washboard in one corner, a couple of saw horses that I would ride, wires strung from the ceiling. Laundry was washed there, then hung to dry from ceiling wires. John Lee's hand laundry smelled of clean and of steam and of Niagara starch in boiling water. Sometimes there would be a loud hiss, and the smell of soy sauce and soybeans and vegetables would pour in from the almost-a-back room. Sometimes a fried egg sandwich for my lunch. Sometimes egg foo yung, when fish-head soup was the specialty for Mom and Dad. Store fronts and store-front apartments, a laundry, a business, Chinese food unlike Chinatown's. This was part of my world, part of America—yet foreign, foreign to most Americans, I'd guess.

In the almost-a-back room: the picture of John Lee's apartment building back in China and a picture of John Lee himself, suit and tie, speaking into a microphone. John Lee was a big shot in the Chinese community (which was larger than Chinatown). Other Chinese launderers seemed to seek his advice. John Lee was a merchant, with a "China-side wife," his own high rise, able to dispense silver dollars on my birthdays and on Christmases and Easters. He was the affluent among the poor. It was a sign of affluence that when John Lee would take us out to a Chinese restaurant, waiters would seat us in the back room among the silk-suited Chinese men and fur-collared Chinese women; a sign of affluence that waiters would bow often, that they would actually write down our order. Mom and Dad could claim none of that.

Mami on the assembly line at Standard Toycraft. Forty dollars a week—a dollar an hour. Dad, a machinist's assistant, then shop steward for a time, as well as working downstairs at Jimmy Vriniotis's deli in the evenings, short order at a greasy spoon. John Lee had more than we. But John Lee was an immigrant. He could never look American (thoughts of a child). He had an accent. So did Mom and Dad, but John Lee's was foreign. He'd say "fly lice" or "loose poke" instead of "fried rice" and "roast pork." He'd call me "Bobby," despite my lessons on calling me "Papi."

There is a point here that I'll get to in detail below. It is that we behave as if the minority problem is the immigrant problem. Two generations of learning the language and the ways of America, and all will be better, we hear. But two generations come and go and all that happens is that the minority's native tongue is gone. The African American lost his native tongue two hundred years ago. More on this too. For now, look to how far the analogy has been drawn. After sociolinguists posited a "language interference" to explain a transitional period in a foreign-language learner's acquisition of a new language, linguists and compositionists posited a dialect interference among Black English speakers (see Hartwell). Learn the language and all will be better, they suggested, a promise to African Americans as well as non-English speakers (e.g., Farrell). Two generations and blacks will melt? We need to look more broadly, historically, to the differences between minorities and immigrants, so as to break from the not helpful analogy between the two in the classroom and in our theorizing.

School.

All Saints, the Catholic school around the corner from Bartlett, across the street from PS 168, the public school. All Saints charges a dollar a month for tuition (three a month in the seventh and eighth grades). It is my school from kindergarten till eighth-grade graduation. There I am filled with Catholicism, "Ave Maria," and with "Jingle Bells," maxims from Poor Richard, laws from Newton, the Beaver's neighbors—Dick and Jane, the parts of speech, times tables. There I play in the melting pot.

Or maybe it was a stewpot. A stew, not the easy mixes of the salad-bowl metaphor, the static coexistence of the mosaic metaphor. The stew metaphor maintains the violence of the melting-pot metaphor while suggesting that some of the ingredients do not lose all of their original identity, though altered, taking in the juices from the other ingredients of the pot, adding to the juices; all of us this one thing, Americans, and all of us some things else; for some of us, never complete integration and never complete integrity. With the stewpot comes the sense that not all the ingredients are equally important, that the stew needs the beef of a Yankee pot roast cut more than fatback or red beans and *sofrito.*

As I saw it, prestige belonged to the Wattses, Andrew and Stephen. There were nuns and priests in their family. They lived in one of the brownstones, around the corner, not of the block. The kids on the block didn't look like the Wattses, didn't talk like them. I don't recall ever thinking they were better, in the sense of superior—they just had it better. And I don't recall ever thinking about what "having it better" meant; I just knew that they did.

There was something special about Jarapolk Cigash and his family too. But theirs was different from the Wattses. The Wattses were connected to All Saints, somehow, to culture, though that word—culture—only occurs to me now. Jarapolk, "Yacko," Jerry, was one of my two best friends (superlatives have no meaning for children). The Cigashes lived in the neighborhood, but there was something special about their apartment: a piano that his sister played; a stand for sheet music alongside a violin case. Jerry practiced the violin. His parents would speak of their escape from the Ukraine, explain what it meant to be a satellite country. They had accents, thick accents, but there was an air about them. They were educated, in that special sense in which *educated* is sometimes used. It was clear to me even then that Brooklyn would only be a stopover for the Cigashes. It was not their home nor would it be. That wasn't clear about the Villanuevas.

I had the sense that there was something different about Charles Bermudez. He was kind of pale, allergic to milk. There was something strange about the way Charles's father held his cigarettes: palm up, the cigarette pinched between thumb and middle finger, like a movie old-world aristocrat or a monocle-wearing fascist general. Yet I didn't see prestige in the Bermudezes, really, just difference. Now as I look back, I wonder if the Bermudezes were Latin Americans on the run. Back then, I just assumed they were portoricans. Portoricans could not be foreign, like the foreignness of the very American Wattses or the foreignness of the Eastern European Cigashes.

Marie Engells, the German girl, was another stopover. We were in school together from kindergarten through the eighth grade, yet I never knew her. Some of that was due to childish gender discrimination, no doubt, though Rose Marie, Peanuts, the Italian girl, was always a special friend, not boyfriend-girlfriend, not one of the boys, and not so as I feared being seen as a sissy, just a special friend. We'd buy each other knishes or soft, salted pretzels from the pushcart after school. But there was something about Marie Engells: an awfully erect back, the hint of a smile constantly on her lips. Maybe all this was in my imagination, but she seemed aloof to me. Marie Engells was the girl valedictorian at eighth-grade graduation. Jarapolk Cigash was the boy. They were immigrants. And something was theirs that wasn't mine. Yet I was American and so were my parents and the generation before them, full citizens since 1919.

Some fell into a grey area between the immigrants and those like me, the spics or the blacks. I knew Peanuts wasn't like us, but she wasn't like Marie Engells or Jarapolk Cigash either. And I was less sure about Frankie Thompson, the Irish kid who introduced me to my first cigarette in one of the neighborhood abandoned lots where we jumped burning Christmas trees every year. I was less sure about Paul Caesar, "the Polack." I was less sure about their advantage despite the same school, the same neighborhood.

They would have been "new immigrants," not as easily assimilable, the bad-element immigrants that prompted the latent footnote to the Statue of Liberty: "in limited numbers." In terms of ethnicity, the Cigashes should have been "new immigrants" too, but pianos and violins suggested maybe these new immigrants came from higher in the class system. Class comes into the academic's thoughts. The child only knew that Peanuts and Frankie Thompson and Paul Caesar were not in the same league as Jerry or Marie Engells, the Wattses, maybe even Charles Bermudez. And it didn't have anything to do with brains. Yet I still believed they had something over Lana Walker and Irving Roach and me.

Irving Roach was the only African American kid I knew who didn't live on the same street I did. The African American kids went to PS 168. "You know we ain't Catholic," I was told once when Hambone said he wished he could read like I did, when I asked why his folks didn't send him to All Saints. Irving Roach didn't live on the block, but was of the block. I had a life on the block—with Butch, the black bully (stereotypes sometimes have bases in fact—Black Butch the Bad-ass Bully, Darnell the Dude, Lazy Leroy, Hambone with the thick glasses and bookish ways), Papo, the PR bully, Mike and Steven Figueroa and Enchi and Hershey. And I had a life at All Saints. And only Juan Torres, Johnny, my best friend from kindergarten till my family moved to California, and Irving Roach crossed over. And Irving Roach was kind, would bring his baby sister with him when he came to visit. And we would talk school things. He was smart. But I don't recall imagining him "making it."

Lana Walker might. She was as aloof as Marie Engells, as smart, too, I thought. And Lana Walker was beautiful, black and slender (but not skinny) and tall. I was short and chubby and all too insecure to do more than talk with her in passing in the nine years we were in school together. At eighth grade graduation Marie Engells would win the math award I really wanted. Lana Walker would get some special recognition, though I no longer remember what. I would get the spelling and the penmanship awards: the Merriam-Webster spelling bee champ that year. Jerry and Marie Engells went to the Catholic college-prep high school. Lana Walker made the alternate list. I never saw Irving Roach again. Juan Torres ended up in the vo-tech school in his area. I went to Alexander Hamilton Vocational-Technical High School.

So what had happened? I was an "A" student, third or fourth in the class, able with language, Saturdays spent on special classes in preparation for the entrance exam to the college prep high school. Why hadn't I made it? Mom says the Bishop's Fund, but that seems inconsistent with a dollar tuition. Cultural bias in standardized tests is the more obvious answer.

I think of cultural bias in two ways. The first is a linguistic and rhetorical bias. It has to do with the test-makers' assumption that words have fixed meanings that are not arbitrary. The psychologist Lev Vygotsky, literary critic Mikhail Bakhtin, the philosopher Jacques Derrida, the archeologist and social critic Michel Foucault, as well as the Sophists of fifth-century B.C. Greece, and a score of others, call this into question, seeing language tied to time and place and culture and even ideology. So do kids who are bilingual and bidialectical. Sociolinguist Fernando Peñalosa sees the code switcher, the bidialectal speaker, as "the skillful speaker [who] uses his knowledge of how language choices are interpreted in his community to structure the interaction so as to maximize outcomes favorable to himself" (quoted in Gilyard 31). In plain English: the code-switcher is a rhetorical power player. He knows language isn't fixed, has a relativistic perception of language, knows that words take on hues of meaning when colored by cognates; and for the bilingual there are words seeming the same in both languages, derived from the same sources, but nevertheless having undergone change through time and place. A relativistic notion of language is bound to be a problem for the standardized-test taker. A solution: English Only. One of the many problems with the solution: better writers have a heightened metalinguistic awareness, an awareness of language's multiplicity (Hartwell). So do the bidialectal and the bilingual. English Only could destroy the very metalinguistic awareness that could make for a better writer. Doomed if we teach to the test: doomed to lose the power of having a greater metalinguistic awareness. Doomed if we don't: doomed to be denied access.

The second way I think of cultural bias in standardized tests has to do with the differences between the minority and the immigrant. The immigrant seeks to take on the culture of the majority. And the majority, given certain preconditions, not the least of which is displaying the language and dialect of the majority, accepts the immigrant. The minority, even when accepting the culture of the majority, is never wholly accepted. There is always a distance.

The minority looked at the immigrants like John Lee and Mrs. Ashell, who had been on the continental United States far longer than his parents, who had some economic advantages (Mrs. Ashell through her Sonny, at least), and still felt they were less American than he. The minority looked at his immigrant school friends, second generation, maybe, and believed that theirs was the advantage.

More recent.

A discussion concerning a minority issue takes place at a national conference. It starts to get heated. One person tells of his sympathy. He says, "After all, we're all minorities in a sense." And in a sense he is right. In a sense. Relatively few these days can claim direct lineage to the majority culture of England. But he misses essential differences between immigrants and minorities.

A writing group in a graduate composition course. Martha Lopez's and Paul Reyes's group-work gets loud, drowning out the rest. Martha: black eyes, thick black hair, an accent to her voice. Paul: pale skinned, green eyed, red haired, no accent. Martha argues that her writing suffers from having learned English through grammar instruction, rather than through real conversation and writing practice. Paul argues that even after learning the language there is still the problem of thinking like white folks. He'd *be* white to anyone's eyes. He's drawing on contrastive rhetoric, the notion that different cultures display different rhetorical patterns in their discourse (more of which later). Yet there is more going on than Paul's contrastive rhetoric contention. Martha is arguing the case for assimilation through learning the language of the majority. Paul is arguing that learning the language isn't all there is. Both are Latinos, Spanish speakers. But Martha is Colombian; Paul is Puerto Rican. Martha, the immigrant. Paul, the minority. Martha believes in the possibilities for complete, structural assimilation; Paul is more cautious.

I think of those who try to calm others by saying that it takes two generations for ghetto dwellers to move on. This has been the pattern for immigrants. But what then do we do with the African American or the Latino, especially the Mexican-American, on American soil, in American society, far longer than two generations? What happens to them—to *us*—those of us who are of color, those of us normally labelled "minority"? The answer, I believe, comes in looking more closely at how one becomes assimilated.

Three factors affect the possibilities for complete structural assimilation:

1. The historical mode of entry into the dominant society;
2. The number and distribution of those attempting to take part in the overall society; and
3. The racial and cultural characteristics of those seeking equity with the majority.

I condense a list drawn by political scientist Mario Barrera. And even these three are interrelated. But let me continue with the convenience of the separation. To begin, if the mode of entry of the new group is voluntary, the new group does not carry the baggage of having become part of America through bloodshed. The bloodshed of the Civil War was the price paid for the admission of all African Americans as freed citizens ("all" because there were free blacks, as well as slaves, prior). Bloodshed marked the relationship to American Indians. There was the blood let at the Mexican War of 1846; at the Spanish-American War, the war which led to the acquisition of Puerto Rico. If the mode of entry is voluntary, the general attitude is that the new folks will attain full citizenship in time because they would most wish to do so (though we know that first-generation folks, especially refugees from war-torn countries, often hold dreams of returning).

If the mode of entry is voluntary, then the numbers entering would not be great enough to cause a threat to the majority. Should race become a factor, the numbers can be legally controlled.

The Chinese were granted only limited access from 1882, explaining John Lee's China-side wife. Limited access also explains attitudes toward Southeast Asian refugees, Koreans, Filipinos (Asian and Polynesian and, often, Spanish-surnamed, and from a former colony).

Among Europeans, the "New Immigrants" were not welcomed with open arms. Liberty's torch of freedom burned low. In 1907, President Theodore Roosevelt appointed an immigration commission to study what was being perceived as an immigration problem. By 1911 the commission issued a forty-two volume report. Its findings were that "new immigrants," Eastern and Southern Europeans, were inherently inferior to old immigrants. The commission cited anthropologist Madison Grant:

> The new immigration contained a large and increasing number of the weak, the broken, and the mentally crippled of all races drawn from the lowest stratum of the Mediterranean basin and the Balkans, together with hordes of the wretched, submerged populations of the Polish ghettoes. Our jails, insane asylums, and almshouses are filled with human flotsam and the whole tone of American life, social, moral, and political, has been lowered and vulgarized by them. (quoted in Estrada et al. 115)

By 1924 there were legal restrictions against the admission of ruddy-skinned Eastern European and Mediterranean new immigrants to the United States.

And so the numbers remain relatively small, the small numbers initially locating in ethnic pockets surrounded by the dominant group, ghettos, with smaller numbers moving out, for the most part, only after having achieved cultural assimilation. That is, if race weren't a factor. Chinatowns remain all through the country. There are fewer Little Italies, I think.

His first professional job, Kansas City. His co-workers, college professors, the middle class, mainly white, say he and his family have moved into the Italian neighborhood. And the old housing projects of the neighborhood do bear a faded wooden imitation of an Italian flag. There is an Italian deli, and the local warehouse supermarket bears an Italian name. But there are no Italians. The neighborhood belongs to the white working class with southern-like twangs to their speech, not Italians but folks claiming rural Arkansas, mainly.

When entry is by conquest, the numbers in the conquered land tend to be greater than the numbers of the conquerors, like the residents of Mexico or New Spain, or like those of Puerto Rico. The restricted landmass of Puerto Rico, a small island, pretty much assured that the numbers could not be turned around in the way the numbers were turned around in parts of conquered Mexico. Since the people are conquered in their own lands, they remain rooted to the land's history and culture.

New Mexico: denied statehood until Anglos outnumber the Hispanics (Conklin and Lourie 67).

Arizona: statehood denied, several times, because of the territory's Mexican "mongrel racial character."

From 1891, the Court of Private Claims overturns one land grant after another, until almost all Mexican landowners in New Mexico, Arizona, California, and Texas are displaced (Utah and Colorado never having had large numbers of Mexican landowners).

1928. Congressional hearings on Western Hemisphere Immigration. There is a concerted attempt at preventing the Mexican migrants from working farms, railroads, and mines, of damming the first wave of Mexican immigration which had begun in 1910 (and which would end in 1930). One speaker before the hearings describes Mexicans:

> Their minds run to nothing higher than animal functions—eat, sleep, and sexual debauchery. In every huddle of Mexican shacks one meets the same idleness, hordes of hungry dogs, and filthy children with faces plastered with flies, disease, lice, human filth, stench, promiscuous fornication, bastardly, lounging, apathetic peons and lazy squaws, beans and dried fruit, liquor, general squalor, and envy and hatred of the gringo. These people sleep by day and prowl by night like coyotes, stealing anything they can get their hands on, no matter how useless to them it may be. Nothing left outside is safe unless padlocked or chained down. Yet there are Americans clamoring for more of these human swine to be brought over from Mexico. (quoted in Estrada et al. 116)

The description lumps the Mexicans with the American Indians ("lazy squaws"), another conquered people. Yet the bad-mouthing does not stop the solicitation of Mexican stoop laborers as long as there is profit in having them—and does not distinguish the Mexican from the Mexican American.

When the Great Depression hits, Mexicans and Mexican Americans who apply for relief are directed to "Mexican Bureaus." The Bureaus' job turns out to be *ex*patriation sold as *re*patriation. Mexicans are herded into cattle cars and railroaded to a home that for many has never been theirs. In 1933, a Los Angeles eyewitness to the expatriation process gives voice to the usual rationale:

> The repatriation programme is regarded locally as a piece of consummate statecraft. The average per family cost of executing it is $71.14, including food and transportation. It cost one Los Angeles County $77,249.29 to repatriate one shipment of 6,024. It would have cost $424,933.70 to provide this number with such charitable assistance as they would have been entitled to had they remained—a savings of $347,468.40. (quoted in Estrada et al. 118)

From 1929 to 1934, the number of repatriated Mexicans exceeds 400,000. Approximately half are native to the United States—expatriated. The conquered (minorities) and the voluntary (immigrants) had gotten mixed.

Nor is the confusion of conquered and voluntary out of the ordinary. Others with the same racial and cultural attributes as the conquered, including language, enter voluntarily and follow the pattern of the voluntary immigrant. Puerto Ricans solicited to work in New York and Chicago and Colorado get mixed with other Spanish West Indians and with Central Americans who voluntarily immigrate to the mainland. The same story for the Mexicans of the Southwest, shipped to Pennsylvania and to the Midwest to work mines and stockyards, for Mexicans of the West solicited to work the farms of California and Washington. All get mixed with the Mexican immigrant. And to the extent that structural assimilation is possible for the immigrant, those of the historically conquered who get confused for the Mexican join in the advantage sometimes. But this isn't the rule. More often, the voluntary share in the fate of the historically conquered.

Southeast Asian refugees suffer the historical fate of the Chinese excluded, the fate of the Japanese interred. Cuban refugees suffer the fate of the Puerto Rican and Mexican American. Haitians are black West Indians—a double whammy. I overgeneralize, I know, but I believe the distinction holds generally.

The voluntary of the same or similar cultural and racial attributes as the conquered share in the fate of the conquered. The depression-era expatriation of Mexican Americans with Mexicans was not an isolated instance. The post-Korean War economic recession saw "Operation Wetback" with 3.8 million Mexicans expelled (Murguía 72). The series of economic recessions which began in the 1970s has seen a resurgence of "green card" checks. The rationale behind repatriation and expatriation involves the too great numbers, and underlying the rationale is the attitude of conquerors over the conquered. The result tends to exclusion rather than assimilation.

Race is the final factor affecting assimilation. The crackdowns on Mexicans in the 30s, the 50s, and the present have immigration authorities checking documents of those who "look Mexican" (Murguía 72). The closer the features of a minority correlate to the general features of the majority, the greater the chances for assimilation (and so the Jewish or East Indian or something-looking—but not Puerto Rican-looking—gets his Ph.D. and gets to write this book).

Tato Laviera, a Puerto Rican poet, describes the problem of race, culture, and language:

> i want to go back to puerto rico
> but i wonder if my kink could live
> in ponce, mayaguez and carolina
>
> tengo las venas aculturadas
> escribo in spanglish
> abraham in español
> abraham in english
> tato in spanish
> "taro" in english
> tonto in both languages (quoted in Flores et al. 214)

Acculturated veins ("*las venas aculturadas*"), yet not American and no longer quite Puerto Rican, linguistically a fool in both English and Spanish ("tonto in both languages"). The minority lives in a netherworld. Not quite American. No home to return to.

While the immigrant tends to become American in two generations, two generations only manages to erode the possibility for migration, for the Puerto Rican's return to the Island, or the Mexican American's (assuming the Mexican American's heritage is not from Mexico's ceded land, Texas and the like, but from present-day Mexico) return to Mexico.

Puerto Rico is not my home. It's my parents'. Some of its cultural ways are mine. Some of its language. But I'm more Brooklyn than anything else. The Nuyorcino, often racially closer to the African American than to the majority, takes on much of African-American culture.

Tato again:

> a blackness in spanish
> a blackness in english
> mixture-met on jam sessions in central park,
> there were no differences in
> the sounds merging inside.

And even when external attributes are not black or mulatto, the merging remains. I no longer speak with a blackness, not without the affected quality of white folks trying to sound black, but it resounds more of "home" within me nevertheless.

The new Teaching Assistant was videotaped. He saw and heard the sounds of a New York Jewish intellectual. He was shocked. Something had happened to the sounds of the Brooklyn boy. Yet he knew his portorican blackness remained within.

Nor am I alone in this. There remains Paul Reyes, the green-eyed, red-haired Puerto Rican who referred to "white folks." There remains the empirical—Paul and I are racially white. So Paul Reyes is a graduate student of English in Northern Arizona—and I am one of his English professors. And together we watch the more blatant instances of racism directed at the American Indians where we live: the conquered, their numbers great in Northern Arizona, near America's largest Indian reservation. And the local Navajos tend to be more racially distinct than Paul is or than I am. We have had chances not afforded other Puerto Ricans because we are racially closer to the majority, because we are not part of Northern Arizona's local memory and lore of conquest, because our numbers are so very few in the mountain city. And yet we know we are not assimilated. We are still "Hispanics," a word which says "other-American."

The immigrant enters; the minority is entered upon. Race and culture, sheer numbers and concentration, how one comes to be American: these are the factors that tell of the degree of melt in the pot. The difference between the immigrant and the minority amounts to the difference between immigration and colonization.

No other theory holds up as well as colonial theory—not theories on biological deficiency nor cultural deficiency nor racial inequality. Biological deficiency theories no longer gather large followings. Few today would listen to the likes of the nineteenth-century Harvard naturalist, Louis Agassiz, who claimed that the brain of the Negro adult "never gets beyond that observable in the Caucasian in boyhood" (quoted in Franklin 3). Still, Arthur Jensen could argue the case that

African Americans are genetically inferior to Whites in 1969 in the *Harvard Educational Review* and again in 1973 in the popular press— *Psychology Today.* And R. J. Herrnstein could provide the same argument in a 1971 *Atlantic Monthly* (see Labov "Academic Ignorance" 59). Thomas Farrell's counter to biological deficiency theories would not be much better. In his version of cultural deficit theory, African Americans suffer a cognitive disadvantage because they reside in an oral culture. His counters would look at relativistic notions of what constitutes cognitive development—different ways of thinking for different social contexts: Scribner and Cole on the social determinants of cognitive functions, Shirley Brice Heath on the unlikelihood of an exclusively oral culture among African Americans, other counters. Biological and cultural deficit theories are not tenable.

Racial inequality theories, on the other hand, do have a kind of merit. They make sense to me. I think, in particular, of John Ogbu's assertion that there are different kinds of minorities, with some minorities suffering a castelike status. For Ogbu there are three different kinds of minorities in America: the castelike, the autonomous, and the immigrant minority. The immigrant minority is clear. Even if she maintains her ethnicity—like, say, Italians often do—the qualities ascribed to her ethnicity are not such that she would be necessarily excluded from the mainstream. The autonomous are those who are subject to ethnic or religious distinctiveness yet manage to accommodate the mainstream, even if not assimilate. Ogbu cites American Jews and Mormons as instances of autonomous minorities. The castelike are those who are regarded primarily on the basis of some particular birth ascription, in this country, race or a particular ethnicity, like Latinos. A while back the media focused less on Jesse Jackson's platform than on his race. Jackson, a castelike minority, was the black candidate. But Dukakis got the more usual coverage. Dukakis was not the second-generation Greek immigrant candidate, except when he himself asserted it. There can be no denying that some minorities cannot transcend their race or ethnicity, even when vying for the presidency of the United States or a seat on the Supreme Court.

For all their worth, however, racial inequality theories have a historical shortcoming. The ideology of racial difference, for instance, is relatively new historically, traceable to the eighteenth century (Barrera 197). African Americans were savages; American Indians, noble savages— culturally inferior, not necessarily biologically. The cultural inferiority (or religious inferiority) of some races determined their suitability for slavehood or other forms of oppression. Racial inequality theory does not explain, for example, why East Indians are considered black by the British but not by Americans. The most suggestive answer: India was a British colony, not an American colony. The American East Indian is more often just another foreigner, another immigrant. Race alone is not the distinctive factor. Race and a history of subservience to those who remain dominant makes for the castelike minority.

Colonial theory refines the concept of the castelike minority by looking to the common feature in the castelike's histories—colonization or colonization's explicitly commodified form, slavery. The autonomous minority holds no memory of colonization in this country. There is no national memory of long-term subjugation of the autonomous minority or the immigrant, as there is of the Puerto Rican, the Mexican, the American Indian, the African American, the Asian (mainly by way of the Pacific Islands, colonies once). Looking to colonization makes a distinction not contained in race alone.

And we can look at present-day colonialism. Political scientists today speak of neo-colonialism, when the colonial power, the metropole, exercises economic control over a colony, saving on having to provide resident military and political forces, using the military only as a final resort. Think of Panama. Think of the Philippine Islands, the former colony granted independence by the United States, but with the United States still managing to mess with Marcos and with Aquino. Then think of the numbers of American minorities who do not enjoy equal status with their peers, even when managing to move within the class system, the many who must remain dependent on financing from the State, the great numbers—an overwhelming majority—of minorities who people the prisons, not because of a pathology but because of money, political prisoners in an economic sense, as then Ambassador to the United Nations, Andrew Young, and then head of "Operation Push," Jesse Jackson, pointed out back in 1978 (Stavrianos 25). There is a kind of neo-colonialism at play right here in the United States.

Minorities remain a colonized people. Sociologist Gail Omvedt sees colonialism as "the economic, political and cultural domination of one cultural-ethnic group by another" (quoted in Barrera 193). And Gonzales Casanova goes a step further, writing in terms of the "domination and exploitation among culturally heterogeneous, distinct groups," thereby accounting for a colonialism even when the colonized live and work among the colonizers (quoted in Barrera 194). Casanova is referring to internal colonialism. Colonial theory—internal colonialism—gives a historical precedent and gives a contemporary explanation for how minorities remain castelike, even when racially white, even when white and an expert, a practicing Ph.D. in the language of the dominant.

Mami believed in the traditional idea of language and assimilation. She and Dad had had English instruction in their schooling in Puerto Rico. It was required, an old-fashioned colonialism. Mami had gone as far as the third year of high school; Dad started high school under the GI Bill but switched to a trade school; still, there was the English of the army, though like most Puerto Ricans, his service was mainly on the Island, segregated forces, with the English coming mainly from the officers who were, more often than not, not Puerto Rican. There hasn't been a Villanueva yet who has completed high school (including the one with the Ph.D. and his twenty-one-year-old, GED-toting son).

Mami tells of her and Dad listening to radio shows in English and trying to read the American newspapers, tells of speaking to their Papi in both Spanish and English from the start. He remembers their insistence that he speak in English, that he teach it to them.

Sister Rhea Marie, his kindergarten teacher, visits his home. She is short, thin, plain, a little gap to her front teeth. She wears the traditional Dominican nun's habit: white starch circumscribing her face, seeming severe, as if it would cut off circulation to her face, topped by a black veil, long white apron in front, long rosary beads marking the contrast. For a many-generationed Catholic home, her apparel tells of authority. Her face tells of kindness.

She visits to speak with his Mami and Dad. And she tells them they should speak to Papi in English because "Victor speaks with an accent." But a simple bit of logic has gotten by the good sister: *they* speak with an accent and the accent is passed on with the English. Victor (always "Victor" before Authority) spoke with an accent *because* they spoke in English. There was no verbal deprivation at play, just a process that takes time, "interlanguage," to use a sociolinguistic term.

It took TV for Papi to discover the ways of white language. Watching TV, he discovered that the dessert-that-there's-always-room-for and the rainbow color weren't pronounced the same. It would be a while longer before he stopped pronouncing the *e* when pronouncing certain words—like a fenc*e*d jard.

Then in college he's told to pronounce the *e* when reading Shakespeare, Donne, Marvell, and the like—wing*e*d steed. And he discovers that the British prestige dialect, the Received Pronunciation, prefers a trilled *r*: the rrain in Spain. He discovers this after having worked at removing the trill from the word *three* back in grrade thrree. His English was better than Sister Rhea Marie knew.

Bedtimes, before my mom started working swing and Dad started moonlighting, was reading time. Stories came from *Classics Illustrated*, a kind of comic book. The *Morte d'Arthur,* stories of King Arthur's court, stuck with me, the illustrations leaping to memory a quarter-century later, when reading Mallory in college. Comic books would be my reading supplement to the end of my teen years, a one-a-day within longer readings. And the readings would include Homer and Shelley and Sir Arthur Conan Doyle. Reading and TV and Saturday matinees filled my time more than anything else. And by the time eighth-grade graduation rolled around, I was a spelling-bee champ. And when the school-sponsored reading stopped, reading didn't. And the accent disappeared, and Spanish no longer came easily, sometimes going through French or through Latin in my head, the languages of my profession, searching for the Spanish with which to speak to my family. Assimilation.

And the immigrant went to college prep. And the minority didn't.

III "Spic in English!"

Tension belies the soft calm of muffled brown in the theater-like assembly room at Hamilton. The day had been filled with rumors of Boys High School coming over for an intermural fist fest, a rumble.

OOO-YEA-OH.

An indiscernible chant from outside, like the sounds of spectators at a British or an Italian soccer game. Inside, thick, black garrison belts come off pant loops, are wrapped around fists. Knucks, store-bought brass knuckles, appear from socks. Penny rolls appear, clenched tightly: "Gonna talk cents to them Boys, boys." Blades appear from nowhere.

The clank of brass bars opening metal theater doors. Bright daylight. City buses line the sidewalk. Hamilton doesn't usually get curbside service. Teachers form two flanking walls. No others in sight while eyes adjust. A teacher directs student traffic toward the buses. Silence. The first second.

The next second, a scene from a pirate movie. A thickness of fighting, belts whirling, no voices, no shouts, only thuds and grunts. A suit tie is pulled from behind, from fashion accessory to garrote, a slam in the ribs that's felt just above the groin, glasses smashed into the bridge of the nose. Get to the bus. The bus rocks; the hiss of the door; movement; distance from the madness. Spring 1964.

Summer 1964. Looking down from the ninth-floor kitchen window of the projects. Debris flying, cars being overturned, flames and the sounds of sirens. Dad should be home from work. Past midnight, Dad arrives to tell of being caught on Bedford Avenue, bricks and molotov cocktails, lying down on the floorboard of the Corvair till a policeman knocks on the windshield to tell him to get the hell out of there. Riots in Bedford-Stuyvesant and later in Harlem. Mami announces that she will not raise another child in New York. Stela is two. Mami rules, though Dad is ruler.

Dad's cousin (or something) lives in California. November 1964: sad and happy goodbyes to Don Victor, la Comai, Gollo, Papo, and others. Mami, Dad, Stela, Papi, and all possessions in the Corvair, heading across country, to Los Angeles, California.

Events of the trip: a near collision, a first exposure to room service and color television, a waitress charging for water, pronounced *water*, not *wahta*. Scenes of a land that is broad and empty, profound contrast to the crowded cluster that is New York.

California. They park in Compton.

It was a cultural vacuum, California. The first Christmas still marks it. Dad's still unemployed, Mom's income barely covers the rent and food; there's a small tree in the living room with toys others wouldn't buy: a doll with only one winking eye, a toy piano without legs, things for Stela. Mom and Dad and Papi forego Christmas. He walks the streets that day—it's sunny and eighty degrees—staring at palm trees. The tropics belonged to Mom and Dad.

Papi was born during a New York blizzard, had passed out from the heat during his one visit to Puerto Rico. Christmas was supposed to be snow and wind, the comforting weight of an overcoat, vapor from nostrils, the smell of steam and the sound of complaining clanks on radiator pipes. Christmas was supposed to be a giant tree in Rockefeller Center, the Central Park folks ice skating below, Gimbel's and Macy's aglow with Christmas tree lights, mechanical elves and reindeer and Santa, giant train sets in the windows. At home, steam and the smells of the big cooking: *pasteles,* Dad making the *carne gisao,* Mami the *masa,* Papi spreading *achiote* on the paper that would be folded into rectangular bundles tied with twine, the bundles boiled. *Turron* for dessert, nougat from Spain. There would be the visit to the *abuela* Doña Teresa or to Tia Fela or to Carlina in Long Island. But this year there were just the immediate four, a forgotten meal, and oatmeal for dessert, and summer in Christmas.

The blacks live in a world separate from him, confined to Watts for the most part, not knowing of portoricans, he figured, not seeing portoricans as somehow the same as they, even when the portorican is white. And he isn't Mexican, what with Mom and Dad's jabs at Mexicans' funny ways with Spanish. And the white kids speak a different language, listen to a music that sounds foreign to his ears— the Beach Boys and Jan and Dean: surfin' safaris and deuce coupes and sloops John D, meaningless.

He tries to be white, kind of, taking the lead of the cultural hybrid in one of the two friends he made in school, Buzz Unruh: hair in the pompadour of the low rider, not the peaked pomp of the white working-class low rider, more the pomp of the Chicano, the Vato, the Pachuco; and Buzz wears Chicano work shirts, Pendletons for status, buttoned all the way not just at the top; Levis instead of starched khakis; modified fenceclimbers, without the high Cuban heels—a white working-class/ Chicano mix. Papi, Victor, follows suit. And the dialect of Brooklyn starts to slip with his attempts at social survival during the peer-importance years of adolescence, even though the peers are two. Yet in his room he listens to the Jazz radio station and plays Tito Rodriguez and Pacheco on his portable record player, the suitcase-like machine with detachable box-like speakers; and he reads *Portnoy's Complaint* and *The Godfather,* stories recalling the mixes of New York, a place he is glad to be away from and a place he misses.

His first school in California is Compton Senior High School. The halls don't look much different from Hamilton. The difference is that Compton seems exclusively African American, none of the poor Irish, the Italians, the Puerto Ricans of Hamilton, not even California's Mexicans. He is alone. But he doesn't remain at Compton High long.

Mom and Dad move the family to another part of town in order to have him be in a better school district. This is different. Single-story buildings linked by concrete trails and clusters of lockers, a large grassy field where PE classes are conducted, a large parking lot where stu-dents—*students*—park their cars and motorcycles and Mopeds. And walking about are boys and girls in baggy short pants and T-shirts, a sea of blond hair and pink faces and blue eyes, assemblies on bleachers facing a basketball court, pep rallies with meaningless rhymes, women in short skirts bouncing about, leading the hyperactive rally, a man in plaid pants among the cheerleaders, himself a cheerleader.

At one assembly, a lone black face speaks to the sea of blond and blue about the time for a "nigro" student-body president, and there is silence and a respectful applause. Blond-and-blue are nicer than the Italian greasers were when we ventured outside the block, but the feeling in the air is somehow no different. No nigro student-body president that year.

He doesn't see the clusters of Mexicans at assemblies. But he does see them around the campus: groups of women in short, tight skirts and black hair teased high, thick black lines encircling large black eyes; the men with toothpicks or matchsticks in the corners of their mouths, thick, shiny black hair combed straight back, dark men dressed in plaid work shirts, white undershirts exposed, khakis with waists worn high, bandannas tied around one leg, shiny pointed shoes. They cluster. And he can feel the bristling when black eyes and blue eyes make contact for too long. And he feels that bristling when he makes eye contact with anyone, blue or black. No "Wazzup?" No "*¿Y que?*" Just loud silences.

First day at Manuel Dominguez Senior High School, a meeting with a counselor. First order of business: a bar of soap and a razor. The first order of business is humiliation. *Que portorro* doesn't have a moustache? His is respectable, neatly trimmed always, never did wear a *chibo,* the little strip of hair from the bottom lip to the chin; never did let the moustache turn into a *chinchow,* the Charlie-Chan like droop below the lipline. He wore his moustache like his father had, like his uncle Diego, like the respectable men of the block, like Zorro. But this is not TV California; it's his new world, and he'll comply. With the now swollen, clean-shaven heavy top lip comes the second order of business, the dress code: shorts must have a pocket, so too must T-shirts, no bare feet—rules for wearing underwear as outerwear, as far as he is concerned. He wears his fenceclimbers, pegged pants, white shirt with tabbed collar, a tie, a jacket, his hair combed back. One dresses for school, not because of a code, just because it is school. He is swimming in foreignness. Third order of business: evaluate transcripts.

He knew there would be no college. Hamilton's consolation prize had been architectural drafting. He had the skills, maybe even the talent. Back at Hamilton, he had taken everything he could to prepare him for the job: carpentry and foundry, electrical design, algebra and trig to qualify for strength-of-materials, strength of materials. He mastered the slide rule (which he supplemented with the abacus that John Lee had given him and taught him to use years back). Back in his Bed-Stuy bedroom he had written to Dietz and to Crane and to American Standard, written of his intention to be an architectural draftsman, asked for brochures and drawing templates, and got them. Mom and Dad had given him a fine compass, dividers, a protractor, high-quality triangles, a desk and a T-square, drawing pens, mechanical pencils. There was the promise of a trade on graduation, and the promise that after seven years as an apprentice he could take the AIA test and become an architect.

Dominguez says architectural drafting requires college. But there would be no college. He had resigned himself. The tests had told him so. Dominguez says only so many of all those shop courses can count toward graduation. Strength-of-materials could be a physics course, but to get credit for physics and for the trigonometry there would have to be geometry and a general science prerequisite. Never mind the "A"; there are rules. Physics and trig can't be learned without geometry, can't be understood without the basics. But he had learned and he did understand. No matter. Six months later he's told he won't graduate on schedule. Seems like he hadn't gotten California history his freshman year. It wasn't offered in Brooklyn. So why is he here?

Lockstep and college prep, except that not everyone goes to college. A drafting teacher gives him a special project: design an extension to the school library. He gets building codes, pulls out his templates, recalls his lessons learned at Hamilton, draws a complete set: floor plans, elevations, specs, the works. Gets an "A"—for mechanical drawing, says the report card, not for architectural drawing. No credit, really. Years later, attempting to convert a GED into a diploma (and being denied), he sees the school library's extension. It's remarkably like the one he had designed. No credit and no cash either.

Lockstep, all prearranged, everything on automatic. The geometry teacher recites lectures while staring at the ceiling, never making eye contact. The English teacher requires two-page stories, literally stories, but no reading. History is dates and dead white guys. And PE assumes everyone knows about flag football and decathlons. The block had been basketball, stickball, and king-queen, a kind of handball. The PE teacher shouts, "Go home and get a haircut! And don't come back till you do!" Papi never goes back.

Yet in the short time he was in Dominguez he did manage to make two friends: Buzz Unruh, the tall, lanky, freckle-faced kid who dressed somewhat like the Mexican kids, and Richard Tifft. Tifft had turned to him when he was first introduced to the geometry class and said, "City dude." They were the only kind words, the only acknowledgment, he received in all the introductions in all the classes. Tifft was an Okie, alone, not living in Bell Gardens with the other Okies, a California minority, alone. Later there would be *The Grapes of Wrath*. Later still, there would be the realization that *The Grapes of Wrath* describes the victims of neo-colonialism, the dispossessed because of economics, though blamed on dust. He was taken in by the Tifft household. Tifft's mother was "Ma," his father was "Tifft." He discovered pork fat and beans, taters and fritters. Kind people.

Then the summer of 1965. The Watts riots, flames and looting and shooting on a scale not even imagined at Bed-Stuy. He sits at the Tifft mobile home on the border of Compton and Watts. Flames light up the sky. The sounds of sirens. The sounds of shots fired. Ossie Davis is on the TV saying "Cool it." Tifft, the father, sits with a rifle across his lap. Says, "Might have to kill us some niggers." And somewhere inside, Papi, Victor, is hurt, frightened, confused. He can't let on that something within him is also a nigger.

Like many a Latino, I was upset by Richard Rodriguez's autobiography, *Hunger of Memory,* but I did understand, because he brought back so many of the memories of Mom's push for assimilation and the loneliness of the "other" in a foreign place, of California, of how we are not meant to be alone, and the lengths we will go to not to be alone. It wasn't the story that upset me. There were too many parallels to my own. It was the melancholy, the ideological resignation, the way he seemed not to see that biculturalism is as imposed as assimilation. Richard Rodriguez had been through the cauldron and had emerged American he said. And, being American, he could no longer be Mexican. Yet there is the tension, the hunger, that runs throughout his writing, throughout his story. It is the tension that has others seek him out to discuss his ideas. If Richard Rodriguez were Richard Wilson he'd have no story to tell; if Richard Wilson were describing someone named Rodriguez he wouldn't have the same fame. He remains the other while espousing the same.

Biculturalism does not mean to me an equal ease with two cultures. That is an ideal. Rather, biculturalism means the tensions within, which are caused by being unable to deny the old or the new. Rodriguez struggles at denying the tension, and when he cannot (his hungering memory), he says that is just how it is; it's okay in the long run. I react differently. I resent the tension, that the ideal is not to be realized, that we cannot be the mosaic or the salad bowl. Nor can we be the melting pot, if that were the preference—any more than Richard Rodriguez is allowed to be the American he wishes to be. Rodriguez is not just the writer; he is the Mexican American writer, the writer of the Hispanic experience, whether he cares for the epithets or not, epithets imposed on him even as he denies them—Mexican American, Hispanic. He's still a chili pepper in the pot, not quite melted, like it or not. Rodriguez's mindset is that of the immigrant, attempting to give up "the old country," but minority status is nevertheless ascribed to him.

Even though Rodriguez's success comes to great degree from his arguing the case for assimilation even as his own assimilation is denied him, he is a success. He is, in fact, the noted writer: well-published, anthologized, interviewed by Bill Moyers, an essayist for the *McNeil-Lehrer News Hour.* What he did—what I did in that tension-filled moment in Tifft's mobile home, have done in the years prior and since—is fall back on that painful, confusing strategy that people of color who succeed employ: what Signithia Fordham calls "racelessness." It is the denial of other-cultural affiliation, a denial of the collective, any collective; it is the embracing of America's dominant ideology, the ideology of individualism.

Fordham describes a phenomenon she calls "fictive-kinship" among African Americans and demonstrates how high-achieving African American students distance themselves from that kinship. She describes fictive kinship as the ways in which African Americans assert the collective through particular dress codes, musical styles, other-cultural trappings. In language, the kinship is demonstrated by terms like "brother," "sister," "blood," by the conscious use of Black English. High achievers tend to distance themselves from the cultural trappings and the linguistic codes of those trappings, very often consciously. This is not the same as "passing," an impossibility for those who are not genetically whiter, who are not like Faulkner's octoroon. It is the recognition that for all the talk of black progress, the race has not progressed as far as certain individuals have. Jesse Jackson or Oprah Winfrey are the exceptions, not the rule. It is also the recognition of the school system, a competitive system which measures individual achievement. Racelessness, then, is the decision to go it alone. And it is most clearly marked linguistically, sometimes even by denying that one is choosing to learn to speak white English, by asserting that one is choosing to speak "correct" English, a notion propagated by linguists who eschew the color or even the prestige of the dominant dialect, labelling it as the value-free standard—Standard American English. E. D. Hirsch calls its written form a "grapholect," a consciously contrived, trans-dialectal form of language which serves a normative function in a multidialectal society. It favors no one, he says. But it is clearly closest to the Standard, and the Standard is most like the language of the white middle class.

Choosing to speak the language of the dominant, choosing racelessness, bears a price, however. And that price is alienation—the loss of fictive kinships without being fully adopted by the white community. "Where is your blackness?" from the one community, and "a credit to your race" from the other. "Where is your *raza?*" from the one and (alluding to Richard Rodriguez) "a child of Mexican immigrants" from the other.

In a sense, I was pushed into racelessness in California. I had been set up not to establish a fictive kinship with Chicanos. I don't know where Dad learned of dialects, but he did go on about them.

> All this talk about dialects is bullshit. Those Mexicans don't talk *dialects.* They talk their own language, a mishmash of Spanish and Indian. We speak *Castiliano* [which he would pronounce cath-til-yano], *real* Spanish, like the kings of Spain.

He wasn't exactly right, historically or linguistically. Both the Mexican's Spanish and the Puerto Rican's really are dialects, neither true to the prestige dialect of four hundred years back. Not only would the Spaniard not pronounce Castilian as he had, but the historical Spanish of the Puerto Rican was Andalusian. Still, his assertion (which he voiced often) shows the degree to which I was taught that the Mexican was not to be regarded as somehow kin to the Puerto Rican, an assertion that the Chicanos and the Vatos made clear at my failed attempts to join the community. *"Mira,"* I'd say, just the way to open a conversation, a phatic device in linguistic jargon. *"¿Mira a que?"* would come the retort, usually accompanied with the flip of eyebrows to a vato brother. *"Oyes,"* they'd say, a phatic device. *"¿Oyes a que?"* I'd say to myself. "Slow down," I'd say when they spoke Spanish. "Slow down," they'd say when I did. And if I spoke of *salsa,* speaking of music, they'd wonder why I was talking about hot sauce. We were different.

"Hispanic" is a convenience created by the Census Bureau. And even as we try to choose our own label, we cannot agree. Some find "Latino" is too much a reference to Latin Americans, different from *mexicanos,* Mexican Americans, Chicanos. None of the terms satisfies the group from northern New Mexico, the actual speakers of something close to Castiliano still. Mexican, Cuban, and Nicaraguan immigrants might have cultural and linguistic similarities, but they also differ. Bilingual Hispanics are not necessarily bilingual in the same languages, not exactly.

He sat in the bleachers at Ebbets Field to watch a Brooklyn Dodgers game. Next to him and his dad sit another portorican boy and his dad. The Giants are up. Bases are loaded, only one out, a batter at plate. The stadium is silent. Suddenly, the black portorican boy next to Papi blurts out, *"¡Mira ese bicho!"* The father barely acknowledges the boy. Papi is shocked. That boy should have been popped in the mouth, at least gotten a scolding. What was that boy looking at anyway? Dad sees the shock on Papi's face, smiles, and explains that for Cubans *un bicho* is a bug, an insect. For the Puerto Rican, the word is a vulgar reference to male genitalia.

Barbara Walters is interviewing Fidel Castro on TV with the help of a translator. She asks Castro to respond to the criticism that he is merely a Russian puppet. Castro gets visibly agitated, angry; his response is long, coming at the translator rapidly. The question is, of course, incendiary. But to fuel the fire, I think, was that the translator had used the word *titere,* literally (in a bilingual dictionary sense), a puppet. For the Cuban and the Puerto Rican, however, the word connotes a smart-alecky kid, a punk.

We Hispanics, Latinos, are a multitude of differences. This is not to argue against bilingual education. Bilingual education, it seems to me, has less to do with language than with a lessening of the chances for alienation, the chance for negating the choice between the collective and racelessness. I mention our differences to point out how we are the victims of racism in being regarded as all alike, this one thing, Hispanics. And the irony for those who fear what some are calling the "browning of America" is that the facile labeling instigates that browning, though not necessarily in the sense of promoting a brown nationalism. We begin to see ourselves as somehow the same, Latinos or Hispanics or Spanish speakers, even when we no longer speak Spanish; we begin to put aside our differences. We begin to form a fictive kinship.

This is how Fordham describes the historical formation of the fictive-kinship system:

> [T]he system was developed partly in response to two types of mistreatment from Whites: the economic and instrumental exploitation by Whites during and after slavery, and the historical and continuing tendency by White Americans to treat Black Americans as an undifferentiated mass of people, indiscriminately ascribing to them certain inherent strengths and weaknesses . . . Black Americans have generally responded to this mistreatment by inverting the negative stereotypes and assumptions of Whites into positive and functional attributes . . . Thus, Black Americans may have transformed White people's assumptions of Black homogeneity into a collective identity system. (56-57)

Because Hispanic or Latino cultures are varied, our dialects different, our racial mixes many, and because our historical exploitation came by way of different periods of colonialism and neocolonialism, not as stark or singular as slavery, our process of forming a greater fictive-kinship system is slower and somehow less complete than the process undergone by African Americans. Yet we do begin to form a collective bond, united in the collective threat of anti-brown racism. The Spanish cable television network, Univision, for example, is careful to represent the various Latinos, Hispanics; yet it is the one station, Latino. The portorican transplanted into California soil today would not likely feel the isolation he felt nearly thirty years ago.

Alone, and with no promise for better proffered by the schools, he drops out and goes to work. Like many who are young and uneducated, his first jobs are with the fast-food industry—hamburgers and kraut dogs and chili dogs and tacos and burritos at the local Bun'n'Run. A year earlier, he would have said a *taco* was the heel to a shoe and a *burrito* was a donkey. Now he could put out fifty tacos in less than a minute. Moving up, he becomes a short-order cook. Mom gets him an interview where she works as a keypunch operator for a computerized accounting firm. He maxes a math test and carries himself well with the interviewer, is hired as a checker, looking for keypunch errors when journal balances don't balance. One of the company's computer operators joins the Navy. Victor is sent to the Honeywell computer operations school in Los Angeles, where he learns to operate a Honeywell H-200, a massive machine that holds 16K of memory. And again there is hope for the future.

But it's 1968. General Westmoreland has whispered into President Johnson's ear that the war can be won, given sufficient manpower. This is before the lottery draft system. All eligible nineteen-and-a-half year olds are to be drafted. He's nineteen and a half in 1968.

Fort Ord, California. A thin, short Filipino in a drill sergeant's hat stands before the new recruits:

> Ip you're worried about Bietnam, don't be. Because you're all gonna go anyway and do your job por Uncle Sam. And. Ip you're worried about being killed, don't be. Because you're all such sorry sacks ob shit, you're all going to die anyway.

The words, accent and all, the sun shining on the sergeant standing on the top step to the wooden, two-story barracks, the ice plant peaking through the floorboards on which the sergeant stands, the heat rising visibly from the tar floor, the dropping of the heart like when an elevator begins its too fast descent, the prickly feeling in the face that says blood is rushing away, all are clearer in memory today than this morning's meal.

Victor is told that if he were to reenlist, sign up for an extra year's service, he would be guaranteed training in the field of his choice. The dropout *knew* he would be cannon fodder. He reenlists for personnel specialist school, to become a nice, safe clerk. He had worked in an office and had a way with language. Twenty weeks later, he leaves California for Vietnam. From Long Binh depot to the Central Highlands. They don't need a clerk, so off to a Fire Support Base as a radio-telephone operator—a grunt. Two months later, the company clerk gets malaria, is transferred to Japan. The PFC is sent back to the trains area, the way station between the FSBs and the base camp, where artillery, the MASH, supply, and the company clerks work. Not safe, but a hell of a lot safer.

There isn't much to say about Vietnam. It was and remains somehow unreal no matter how real. Yet, two events mark that year that need mention here. One was the offer to go back to base camp to take the GED exams. The future is abstract enough for a nineteen-year-old, decidedly more so in a war, when mortality becomes all too concrete. I took up the offer because base camp meant ice cream, a steak, and a movie. I did not suffer any test anxiety because I had no future hinging on the test results. Turns out I did well enough to be the equivalent of a high-school graduate. The other event—the greater event—was in finally being back among *portorros,* back among portoricans from the block.

And the startling event within that event was when the Japanese American company commander shouted to us (as we huddled in our bunker) that we were in the American Army and that we *would* speak English, even in private. The order was beyond my understanding, especially in its having come from one who was a racial minority, one whose ancestors may have been confined to American concentration camps, whose ancestors had been nearly obliterated from the face of the earth by America only a generation back. Now I see that the order came from one who had succeeded, one who had taken the path of racelessness, one who would impose racelessness on us all.

More than two decades later another Japanese American (Japanese Canadian, really) would impose alienation. He would push for a change in the American constitution that would insist on English. Back then, I thought that what I spoke among my friends should be of little consequence—there was an American war, and I was in it. My loyalty was surely not at issue; I was more loyal, as I saw it, than the white kids who spoke no language other than English but were burning flags. And many years later I would think that what I spoke among my friends—what little Spanish I had left—should be of no matter. I was an English professor, more able with English than many, maybe most, of the students who spoke no language other than English. The commander's name was Yamashita. The legislator was the late S. I. Hayakawa.

Hayakawa was a Canadian who had come to this country in the 1930s. By the 1940s he had become a leading name in linguistic research. His 1941 *Language in Action* became required reading for most English majors for a couple of decades after. He had been a university president and a United States senator. And he had been the initiator of the English Language Amendment. He had written about how he had been denied an extended stay in America because he was Japanese, even if a native of Canada ("Why the English Language Amendment" 14). Yet he failed to see the racist connotations and ramifications of the drive he initiated. He even went on record with the assertion that Hispanics want a separate Spanish-speaking America. He quoted a handful of the nineteen-sixties Latino fringe ("Official Language" 36–37). So, with John Tanton, a midwestern ophthalmologist, he got the ball rolling. Now there are over seventeen states with English Only laws.

I don't believe that Senator Hayakawa's intent was essentially racist, however, any more than Captain Yamashita's (Hayakawa's alarm over a few Spanish speakers' nationalism notwithstanding). I believe Hayakawa's motives were grounded in a concern for this nation and its people. He believed in the power a command of the English language can wield in this country, the power that a historically English-speaking nation has long enjoyed. Former Senator Huddleston succinctly summed up the belief shared by Hayakawa, and countless others apparently, given the relative success of the English Only movement. Huddleston spoke before a special subcommittee of the Senate Judiciary Committee on English-language legislation:

> For over 200 years, the United States has enjoyed the blessing of one primary language that is spoken and understood by most of its citizens. The previous unquestioned acceptance of the language by immigrants from every linguistic and cultural background has enabled us to come together and prosper as one people. (15)

Prosperity came from the linguistic melt. That makes sense.

But it just isn't true historically. The prosperity, yes, but not quite the acceptance of English. The colonists brought Dutch and some Swedish to the New York-Delaware area, for instance. The Holland Tunnel and Rutgers University remain as reminders. The Huguenots brought French to Louisiana, an officially bilingual state to this day. The Spaniards brought Spanish to Florida, the Southwest, and the West. Germans brought their language to Pennsylvania. Pennsylvania "Dutch" (really Deutsche) remains a distinct dialect, its German influence still present. I have eaten *frankfurters* with *kraut* and mustard since long before *kindergarten*. We are full of German. It is American— not "ethnic," like, say, tacos or Spanish rice or the *barrio*.

Germans did not quietly accept the primacy of English. Those who were in America during the Revolutionary War era were in no hurry to learn English. They prompted Benjamin Franklin to ask in the spirit of present-day English Only advocates,

> Why should the *Palatine Boors* [Germans] be suffered to swarm onto our Settlements and, by herding together, establish their Language and Manners, to the Exclusion of ours? Why should *Pennsylvania,* founded by the *English,* become a Colony of *Aliens,*

who will shortly be so numerous as to Germanize us instead of
our Anglifying them? (quoted in Conklin and Lourie 69)

His answer, it turned out, was that those Boors should be suffered
because a greater unity could be had in pluralism than in subjugation.
The Germans would be necessary allies in a revolution. So, government
documents were published in German. After the Revolutionary War,
during the drafting of the Constitution, the new nation's designers still
decided not to legislate the use of English, despite the perceived threat
of a German primacy. The nation builders believed that principles of
freedom should include linguistic freedom—even the freedom to speak
what the Fathers believed to be an inferior tongue (Heath, "Language
Academy").

German became America's semi-official second language, with even
some instances of official German. In 1795, Germans petitioned the
new congress to have laws published in German as well as English.
The petition of the Virginia delegation made it through committee,
falling to defeat by only one vote. In the years between 1830 and 1890,
4.5 million more Germans came to the United States. Seven years
after the first wave, 1837, Pennsylvania legislated that the public schools
be conducted in English and German—legislated that German would
have equal status with English. By 1840, Ohio's public schools were
bilingual—German-English. Some schools in Minnesota, Maryland,
and Indiana were taught exclusively in German (Fallows). Publicly
funded German schools existed through much of the nineteenth century
(Conklin and Lourie).

The schools did not completely die out until the first world war.
Anti-German sentiment produced legislation after legislation forbidding
bilingual education in German and English, some forbidding German
even in private. The German Americans quieted, assimilated (nearly
two hundred years after their first arrival). Their ancestry had made
them enemies to many here during the war.

After the first world war the push for "100 percent Americanization"
saw bilingual education give way to something like the current teaching
of English as a Second Language. Mexican Americans, along with other
minorities, were included in a nationwide push at Americanizing the
"immigrant," a push with remarkable similarities to the present day.
The California Commission on Immigration and Housing, for example,
outwardly declared its endorsement of "Americanization propaganda"
(Fallows 378). The propaganda campaign evidently worked, given
Huddleston's and so many others' belief in a monolingual American
past.

Among those being compelled to Americanize were not only Mexicans, but the "new immigrants" as well—the Italians, Yugoslavs, Poles, Rumanians—who were living in ghettos. They were inherently inferior, said the anthropologist Madison Grant and public sentiment. The public believed they were refusing to learn English (Hakuta). Does all this sound familiar?

Intensive English instruction was mandated and instituted. Penalties were imposed on those who spoke other languages. Successful learning of English was gauged by students' abilities to speak like the Anglo middle class. The success of these programs was measured by standardized achievement tests and IQ tests, just like today. These and other criteria determined students' high-school curricula, with racial minorities and immigrants consistently finding their ways into trade-oriented schools—schools like Alexander Hamilton Vocational-Technical High School—rather than college preparatory schools.

By the 1930s, English oral proficiency had become a precondition for immigration. English literacy had become a precondition for voting, a requirement also aimed at Southern Blacks, who were neither immigrants nor bilingual. Language-as-unifier has been used to exclude before.

The argument goes that now the numbers are great; too many can live in Spanish-speaking or Tagalog-speaking or Vietnamese-speaking ghettos, self-contained communities. That may be, but that doesn't mean that parents don't want their children to learn English. Of Latino parents who took part in a 1985 national survey, for instance, 98 percent believed it essential for their children to learn to read and write "perfect" English (Hakuta). Latinos are not in positions of power as a people. That there have been only two Latinos in presidential cabinets in two hundred years (both within the last administration, George Bush's)—only two, despite Latinos having been on this country's soil longer than any other European group—illustrates our relative lack of power. And even if *any* non-English-speaking group had sufficient power to undermine America's English primacy, what profit would there be in it? English is the global *lingua franca*.

The chairman of the PLO sits, traditional headgear wrapped around his head and draped over combat fatigues—the nationalist, one we have sometimes called a terrorist. He speaks to a PBS newsman in English. He assumes the language of the journalist, rather than insist on the pose of the nationalist who regularly draws global attention.

PBS television's *The Story of English* notes that the crew of an Air Italia commercial jet, flying over Italian air-space, making a routine local run within Italy, piloted by Italians, speaking to a ground crew which is exclusively Italian, must nevertheless speak in English.

The World Council of Churches has English as its ecumenical language (McCrum, Cran, and MacNeil 20).

English is even the language of the cosmos: Vulcan One's message, representing the people of Earth, approved by the 147 members of the United Nations, is recorded in English (McCrum et al. 19).

Americans attending schools, watching TV, venturing outside their neighborhoods cannot avoid learning English. Even if some did resist, they could not stop the wave of English that would engulf them.

At best, English Only legislation is unnecessary. It provides nothing to foster a faster language-learning rate than people's abilities will allow. English Only laws provide no new schooling. Instead, they are being used to end bilingual programs. Children, in particular, will have to sink or swim. We're told that's how it used to be. But it wasn't. Even the 100 percent Americanization push provided something like ESL.

What's worse, "sink or swim" suggests a resignation to let some sink. Too many already do. And when they do, they don't tend to blame a system that fails them; they tend to blame themselves. Those who swim all too often find they have lost sight of their original homelands, that they hunger for the memory. Some neither swim nor sink: alienated from the first culture, not quite a part of the new culture, "tonto in both languages." Better to have two cultures than one, two than none—no matter the tensions. English Only equals sink or swim equals alienation, whether sunk or swimming or lost at sea.

English Only legislation is also racist, sometimes explicitly. I might grant the late Senator Hayakawa high motives, but I cannot grant Hayakawa's partner, co-founder of U.S. English, similar motives. John Tanton was exposed as declaring that he feared a Hispanic takeover, a takeover by fast-breeders faithful to a Roman Church which does not respect the division of church and state (e.g., *The Christian Science Monitor,* 27 Oct. 1988, 5). He had said that America is going to face "the first instance in which those with their pants up are going to get caught with their pants down" (Wingert 22). There is no way to ameliorate these words. They're racist.

Nor is Tanton's an isolated case.

In Massachusetts, a flier from that state's English Only organization warns that unless English Only efforts win support and gain funding, "White children may be taught that they are descendants of European ice people whose lack of skin color identifies them as an inferior race," that bilingual educators will "do away with English and anything

European," with students "learn[ing] that Western civilization is a cheap imitation of the true source of world culture, Africa" (Atkins 4). This isn't even limited to anti-Latino sentiment, since Spain, the source of so much of Latino cultures, is still in Europe. In this case, official English legislation has been reduced to black and white.

There's the story from Colorado, in which a restaurant manager fired a waiter for having translated a menu item for a foreign patron.

Or the one from Arizona, in which a parole-board hearing was canceled because the would-be parolee required a translator.

The General Accounting Office has even documented cases of discrimination against workers who speak English with a "foreign" accent, with Latinos being three times as likely to suffer such discrimination as others (Califa).

Some, like Senator Hayakawa, I figure, are no doubt well-intentioned in seeking English Only legislation, but English Only legislation can nevertheless be used to further racism, to invade privacy, to constrain free speech, to deny equal treatment under the law. In short, English Only legislation can be used to violate the First and the Fourteenth Amendments to the Constitution. At bottom, English Only legislation is un-American in the best sense of "American," and too typically American in the worst sense—morally and historically.

Whatever Captain Yamashita's angry invective, we continued to speak in Spanish. Look outside the bunker. See if anyone's around. Speak quietly, nearly in whispers. Speak Spanish. We are Spanish, though not one of us would deny being American.

We were like all the rest of the GIs, nostalgic about "back in the world." "California Dreaming" was probably the most-played song in Vietnam. Our "world" wasn't California; it was *el bloque.* Our world included the portorican Spanglish of the block. The block would not be denied. We didn't say "back in the world." We and the African Americans talked about "back on the block."

Twelve months in Vietnam. Victor returns. Back to the world. But not the block. He's stationed in Stockton, California, an army depot, mainly civilians, with just a handful of military. He marries the woman he had met shortly before entering the army. Marriage is a desperate attempt at continuity, picking up where normalcy had been disrupted by the bizarre. That marriage won't last long. Apart from having to wear a uniform during the days, having to get a haircut more often than he'd like, his life is good in central California, even affluent by his standards. His pay is good; he lives in large family quarters, enjoys the especially low cost of foods at the Commissary, the low cost of civilian medical care. His is an administrative job among civilians. The advantages of the military, without most of the drawbacks. And he and his wife are soon to have a baby. And during the three years he's been in the service the computer field has undergone a boom, computer jobs being filled by college graduates. But he's just a GED. He reenlists.

IV Coming to a Critical Consciousness

"I'm not paid to think," spits the sergeant first class, red-faced, nose-to-nose with Sgt. V.

"Well, you sure earn your keep," comes the calm response from the too-young staff sergeant, the response from one who is supposed to be a peer to the sergeant first class, a fellow lifer.

He had always annoyed Sergeant First Class Priest. He wasn't enough of the soldier, of the NCO, for the sergeant first class's taste. And what made him all the more annoying was that he was good at his job, at personnel administration—got the job done well, special kudos from the Inspector General's office, continually qualified for special proficiency pay. That was annoying, coming from one who lacked even a modicum more than the army's minimum requirement of starch, spit, and polish. Even more annoying was that even though he didn't look quite the ideal soldier, he toted the symbols of the ideal: the decorations of combat, the accelerated promotions of combat. Even at twenty-six, his age when he would have his fun taking jabs at SFC Priest, he was too young to be a staff sergeant, only one rank below this man who was approaching retirement. His very presence could push the Sergeant's cliché button.

He had only been in the army seven years, not even half-way to retirement, when he found his greatest skills were in pushing the buttons of the SFC Priests. Playing with language. But this tires quickly. Having no choice about where to live for how long or with or without family tires quickly too. And he likes his most recent duty station, the Pacific Northwest. It beats Los Angeles. It beats Brooklyn. It's time to get out. Nor is this a spur-of-the-moment decision: it had been building for some time.

Thoughts of doing something other than career military probably started in Stockton, California, shortly after reenlistment. Thoughts of something other likely began with the assignment of Private First Class Walter Myles to the personnel office where he worked.

Walter Myles was an African American draftee who had declined an offer to attend Officer Candidate School because he would do no more than the two years of service required by law. Walter was short, of medium build, balding slightly, with horn-rimmed glasses, and a pipe smoker. Nothing remarkable about his appearance. But there was a calm confidence in his bearing, bad without being bad-ass. Sgt. V had never met an African American like him before: one who could clearly hold his own, yet not given to bippin' or boisterousness, one whose Black English seemed somehow to have a prestige register to it. Walter Myles was Sgt. V's first friend who was a college graduate of color: a BA in psychology, no sports scholarships, from Palo Alto, a West-Coast ghetto, "Little Nigeria."

Together they would listen to Miles Davis, "Hot Buttered Soul," poke fun at Mr. Spock's kind of logic on *Star Trek,* swap stories about "gettinnover" as children in the ghetto. Walter introduced him to the family, a large family in a single-family dwelling in the ghetto. Walter introduced him to college cronies, other African Americans who, like Walter, spoke in abstract political terms and in generalized terms about racism and the struggles of people of color, who spoke like academics but in the language of the streets, kind of—calm, unaffected, intellectual Black English.

The artist breaks into lecture, trying to explain his philosophy to Walter's portorican friend from the Army. He says something like

> The problem is that the Afro-American artist can't get his socio-political shit together. Y'dig? They're like Booker T. Washington. Just show what you can do without overt racial representation or even overt racial aims. Dig that. Others doing Langston Hughes. I mean, as if we're all middle-class Americans. You see, but where I'm coming from is that Afro-American art should take the risk of being ostracized. I mean black art for social action against white oppression. You hear what I'm saying? Dig where I'm coming from? The problem with *that* is that liberal whites think it's hip, so they collect the art and don't hear the real deal!

The words are not exactly the ones he heard then, of course; Sgt. V didn't understand much of what was being said; but the essence and the sound, the "dig thats" and "hear what I'm sayings," would pop into memory again and again over the years, as notions of the middle class and color would be confronted in his own life, as he would consider those who would espouse certain political sensibilities more out of a kind of chic than a real commitment, out of political correctness more than political consciousness. At the time, however, all he knew was that he was being addressed with a respect he had never before known. And that these were men from the block who had managed, it seemed to him, to keep the block while getting college degrees. They were educated and still black, not raceless.

None demonstrated education without racelessness more than Walter's friend, Bracy. Bracy was black, dark black, thin waisted, wide backed, muscular, the build of a middleweight boxer, black beret, black sunglasses, bare chested, except for a string of teeth. In public, a clenched, black-gloved fist in the air: "Say, blood" or "They it is," nothing more.

From the living room of his quarters, Sgt. V could only see his wife open the entrance door—and watch her blanch, take an involuntary half-step back. "Must be Bracy."

In private, Bracy would speak of the children of Ham, and how that biblical story had provided an ideological justification for the oppression of black people, of how this might have been necessary for the survival of Old-Testament Jews, but the God of the New Testament would be appalled by any idea of second-class peoples. Bracy talked history. Bracy talked about the myth of evolution; in this case, that African Americans or any other people of color would do better in time, saying, rather, that time changes nothing, only people make for change—the message of Martin Luther King's "Letter from Birmingham Jail," though Sgt. V had no way of knowing that then. All that Sgt. V knew was that there was a kind of education possible that had to do with more than just getting to good pay: education as a way of attempting to make sense out of the senseless, to become more, rather than to become other. Bracy had become more black, in a sense.

I would think of Bracy and Walter Myles and the men from Palo Alto University again later, during an ethnographic research study I would take part in. The study concerned an African American educator's attempt to promote a Freire-like pedagogy in a school designed exclusively for students who had been locked out of the public schools, mainly by the court system. His was an overtly political, overtly black, African as well as African American perspective. The study was conducted strictly, following the methods of naturalistic observation, with triangulation provided by three observers, field notes, video and audio recording. In the end, I believe Floyd, the teacher, failed in some important ways. But he did provide me with an education on the problems in attempting the overtly political in an American school, even among a student population with first-hand knowledge of the ways the political system can work against certain groups.

Floyd was an African American poet of some note in the Midwest. His poetry was political, radical, though he claimed not to be Marxist or black nationalist. He had been to much of Africa, had taken part in the literacy campaign in Nicaragua and the campaign in Grenada, had met with Paulo Freire. He worked at the Writer's Project in the midst of a midwestern black ghetto and taught political science at a nearby community college. He had grown up in the neighborhood where the Project was located, had gone to the same schools as his students, had seen the schools and the neighborhood deteriorate. He had been to the city's state university, a campus surrounded on three sides by a large African American community, yet having relatively few African Americans enrolled. He had seen his world as the Third World: colonialism at the heart of the heart of the Empire.

His teaching was based on Paulo Freire's ideas. At the heart of Freire's work is *conscientizacao,* "critical consciousness." Critical consciousness is the recognition that society contains social, political, and economic conditions which are at odds with the individual will to freedom. When that recognition is given voice, and a decision is made to do something about the contradiction between the individual and society's workings against individual freedom, even if the action is no more than critical reflection, there is *praxis.* The way to arrive at critical consciousness, for Freire, is through *generative themes.* Generative themes are critical assessments of *limit-situations,* the myths that maintain the status quo. More simply put, Freire would have students look at their individual histories and cultures and compare those histories and ways of being with what they are led to believe is their place in the world, making the contradictions between their world views and the official world views explicit. This is the dialectic between the subjective and the objective, the stuff known from within and the stuff from external forces.

Freire juxtaposes two philosophical schools, the existentialism of a Jean-Paul Sartre and the structuralism of a Louis Althusser, to arrive at the heady term of *problematizing the existential situation.* Simply put, existentialism says that the essence of being human is individual freedom. Structuralism says that there are social, political, and economic systems in place that keep us from changing the way things are, systems that keep us from fully exercising our freedom, systems that we see as "natural." The way out of these systems is through the *problematic,* by questioning the things we don't normally question, questioning just how natural the "natural" is. Freire would have his students look to themselves, their own experiences, in order to question.

So Freire's process begins with private, lived experience. These experiences are generalized. In generalizing personal events, students find that nothing is value-free, that all is in one way or another political, is always affected by and affecting their conduct as citizens of the various communities they travel within and through. Students discover that they are constantly in dialectical relationships with their environments and that these environments are affected by social, political, and economic circumstances and events. Personal lives must contend with social, political, and economic situations. For Freire, the more students are aware of the dialectic, the more they can affect changes in their selves and in their environments. Individual desires and the ability to meet those desires are not simply dictated by the individual's tugs at his bootstraps, nor are they simply matters of luck. This is what Floyd would have his students know from a decidedly black perspective.

Floyd taught writing in the Writer's Project of a midwestern, not-for-profit private school aimed exclusively at low-income adolescents and young adults who had been locked out of traditional public schools but wanted back in. During the two semesters that I conducted the research there, only one white kid had been enrolled, no Latinos. The students were almost exclusively African American. The Executive Director stayed out of curricular matters, focusing instead on generating money with which to keep the school alive. Floyd could do Freire without the kinds of institutional constraints American teachers tend to have to face.

In class, Floyd talked of history and of culture. He said that the idea of black progress was deceptive. Blacks had not simply risen from slavery; they were an ancient people, once great. He told of Christopher Columbus's diary describing black Africans returning home from what Columbus had not yet discovered. He played Charlie Byrd's "You Wear the Crown" on a ghetto blaster, the refrain saying "Imhotep was you and me." Floyd showed that there were black cultures and black history before there were black Americans.

Floyd not only spoke of history and culture but also of ideology. He told students that as members of the Writer's Project they were meeting something of a cultural imperative. He said that lower- and middle-income blacks are members of a culture of oppressed people. They would have to think of themselves as such. He outlined four preconditions for "the true progress of oppressed people":

1. the creation of history;
2. the raising of a mass consciousness to oppression;
3. the refusal of the people to accept oppression; and
4. the rising of the conscious intellectual.

He repeated the preconditions often, but he never explained them, even when asked by me, saying that they're pretty much self-evident. I wanted to know how he had arrived at these preconditions. "Later." But later would never come, just be passed on to another later. My guess is that he had drawn an analogy between the ways some political theorists discuss the class system and culture or race.

It's hard to discuss the class system in America, because for so long we believed that ours was a classless society. John Kenneth Galbraith believes that most Americans still hold to the notion and cites George Bush as saying that class is "for European democracies or something else—it isn't for the United States of America. We are not going to be divided by class" (30). Yet *Business Week,* surely not a magazine critical of capitalism, has to acknowledge on the cover of its August 10, 1992, issue that there had been a "widening [of] the gulf between rich and poor." This is surely a matter of class. Yet not even this kind of acknowledgment can account for internal colonialism: the ways in which certain groups, John Ogbu's castelike minorities, can't get around their birth ascription, like having a man who can climb to the point where he can run for president of the country and speak of the same things as other presidential candidates, and still be labeled the black candidate. So there is the class system and there is another system within it that concerns race and culture. Freire does not address the racial, but he does suggest that the transformation that the critically conscious are to generate is the transformation of the class system, since those we call the marginalized are not in the margins of class but are within the structure—at the bottom. In Freire's words:

> They are not "beings outside of"; they are "beings for another."
> Therefore the solution to their problem is not to become "beings
> inside of," but men freeing themselves; for, in reality, they are
> not marginal to the structure, but oppressed men within it.
> Alienated men, they cannot overcome their dependency by "in-
> corporation" into the very structure responsible for their depend-
> ency. There is no other road to humanization—theirs as well as
> everyone else's—but authentic transformation of the dehuman-
> izing structure. (*Cultural Action* 11)

The concept of "the alienated man" comes from Henri Lefebvre, an existentialist Marxist. The alienated man is one who is kept from seeing the whole picture, and in being kept from the whole, the totality, is kept from attaining his humanity, a realization of freedom. Nor is he peeping in from the sidelines, trying to find his place. The metaphor of the margin is neat for teachers of writing, a notebook metaphor where teachers too can often see themselves (e.g., McQuade), but it is potentially delimiting, not providing for the differences between teachers and students. It can keep eyes focused on a piece of paper, not on Freire's "dehumanizing structure," where the alienated are trying to look up from their places at the bottom. Talk of margins and borders is in keeping with Galbraith's belief that the American middle class works hard at denying its dependence on the underclass to maintain its level of comfort. Talk of margins and borders is in keeping with the need to acknowledge what can't be denied, while denying that it is structural. The dehumanizing structure mentioned by Freire involves class and something like a caste system, those whose histories tell of colonization or slavery.

Floyd apparently believed that the processes by which castelike systems can be changed are much the same as the processes necessary for changing class structures. Three of the four elements in Floyd's scheme explain the dynamics of class, the fourth looks to the individual within castes. Three follow the pattern described by Erik Olin Wright in *Classes*: class formation, class consciousness, and class struggle. The fourth follows Antonio Gramsci's notion of the organic intellectual. Together, they follow Freire's juxtaposition of the individual and the social. Floyd was throwing his students into some deep political waters.

Let me explain. "The creation of history" would be likened to "class formation," which tells of how groups come together over time, historically. This is something more than culture in the usual anthropological sense. It is not enough to recognize and make explicit our cultures. We need to recognize cultures in the context of other cultures, since none of us can be mono-cultural in America. Mexican Americans may have a culture in common with many Mexicans, say, but Mexican Americans also have culture in common with fellow Americans. Their relation to the Mexican can become antagonistic when they favor the American inordinately, as in a Richard Rodriguez; the Mexican American nationalist would likely face as much opposition as a Rodriguez. Puerto Ricans may be "Hispanics," yet our history in general and our history as it pertains to the United States is very different from the histories of both the Mexican American and the Mexican. Nuyorcinos are also Puerto Ricans, but we are in many ways culturally closer to African Americans than to Mexicans. Histories tell of the formation of a class of Mexican Americans, and they tell of the class of the Puerto Ricans of the Island, and they tell of the Puerto Ricans of *el bloque*. Hispanics all, yet different in their ways, their histories, their relations to other Americans, whose cultures and histories they also share to great extent. Such histories are not the standard of the schools. The histories need to be re-created.

The second element in Floyd's kind of class structure is class consciousness. It's achieved when a class recognizes its ideologies, its world views. This gets complicated for Americans of color in much the same way as their histories do. I grew up eating rice and beans and thinking Teddy Roosevelt was great, never considering that one of the things that made him great was his establishing Puerto Rico as an American colony. Now I consider the reasons why Puerto Ricans remain the most disadvantaged of American Hispanics. And I continue to enjoy the stories and myths of Teddy Roosevelt (liking the Teddy of *Arsenic and Old Lace* best). Americans of color, in particular, cannot accommodate the ideological contraries we carry until we can recognize that we contain cultural multitudes which are sometimes opposed. Terms like "African American," "Asian American," "Mexican American," etc. can tell of a biculturalism in some ideal sense. But they tend not to. They tend to tell of an antagonism between cultures, at least a tension. The antagonism needs to become conscious, not just a latent memory.

Class struggle concerns conflict. It concerns the point in which, in Floyd's terms, the oppressed refuse to put up with oppression. Floyd has his students take part in an anti-apartheid rally, a gesture at political action, a gesture extending students' senses of racial oppression beyond this country. For Freire, just giving voice to the consciousness is struggle, is action, is praxis.

The extension of racial awareness leads to the fourth element in Floyd's scheme: the creation of the conscious intellectual. This comes from Gramsci, of whom I'll have more to say later. For now, it is enough to note that Gramsci writes of the organic intellectuals who would be the voice of the oppressed class of which they are a part. The students at the Writer's Project, according to Floyd, were potentially those conscious intellectuals. In Floyd's words:

> So, for oppressed people to make progress, people like you are necessary. You have an important role. You're like the fuse on the dynamite. If you don't go anywhere, the people don't go anywhere. So the propaganda I'm laying out to you this morning is that if you change your self, you will change the people and, in fact, change the world because you're influential. You can talk. You can write. People listen to you frequently. . . . You are leaders of a sort.

Remember that Freire would have his students realize the contradictions which are parts of their lives. To the extent that Floyd discussed black history in both American and global terms, and to the extent that he included middle-income African Americans as among the oppressed, he was playing out the contradictions which underlie his preconditions for "true progress."

Within the last of the preconditions, the creation of the conscious intellectual, Floyd placed the emphasis on language. As I'll make clearer later, the organic intellectual is a *rhetor,* a conscious user of language. Floyd's students can be conscious intellectuals because they are discursive. The power of the conscious intellectual is in discourse: talking, writing, listening. For Floyd, as for Freire, as for Gramsci, as for Marx, a "revolutionary act [is] an act of criticism with an eye to the practical" (Wilkie 233). The project's participants were to see themselves as *griots,* Floyd said, oral historians, "young installments in a long train of people who can tell the stories of black people and how we see the world."

In this, Floyd echoed the black nationalism of Marcus Garvey, whom Cornel West has labeled a "proto-Gramscian" ("Marxist Theory" 20). Gramsci had thought that a collective black sensibility might be necessary for black Americans to affect change, this by "giving the African continent a mythic function as the common fatherland of all the negro peoples" (21). Floyd had talked to the students about histories and cultures, ideologies and changes.

He had raised their sense of worth. And he did introduce students to the word. His method of teaching composition, however, tended to fall on the side of tradition. He distrusted conventional writing-process pedagogy, even after attending the Bay Area's writing project. He would have good reason. Hegemony can operate by promoting the dominant's ideologies as universal. Process approaches to writing instruction are too often discussed in universal terms—*the* writing process. Process approaches have given rise to cognitive explanations of writing, and the cognitive sciences are also given to claims of universality. Cognitive explanations rendered basic writers, most often members of minority groups, cognitively dysfunctional. The cognitive was extended to the social, and what emerged was Thomas Farrell's claim that African American youth reside in an oral culture, followed by the assertion that as long as those from an oral culture remain oral they would be incapable of reaching Piaget's level of formal operations, the ability to form abstract concepts. Floyd was explicitly aware of Farrell's oral-culture hypothesis (though not of the counters to Farrell). And there was Floyd's skepticism concerning just how much of the nuts-and-bolts of writing could be learned through process approaches, a skepticism common among those who first encounter process approaches (see Delpit). Floyd had an assistant manage drills-for-skills workbooks with his students. Yet he did not completely dismiss writing-as-process.

His was not strictly a product approach to writing. There were drafts and discussions about drafts. But there was no talk in writing-process jargon: no talk of heuristics, brainstorming, clustering. Floyd would not speak of prewriting. He spoke, rather, of art following function, a kind of Aristotelian idea of having something to say, then finding the appropriate artistic garb with which to adorn that something. The art was most often poetry for Floyd. The function he most envisioned for his students' art was structural change. A recognition of the need to instigate structural change would produce writing.

And some of Floyd's students had produced art. One student claims not to go to bed until he has written in his journal. In class, a student reads "The Fatal Disease of Illiteracy," a poem. It tells of the powerlessness in a father who cannot read to his children. Another student, a car thief, a twenty-year-old high school sophomore, writes a poem about the struggle of writing. A couple of the lines read, "Get to it and to it / Till I get it right." Revision was not a stage or a dimension; it was the imperative for effectiveness. To watch Floyd move those he moved was inspiring.

He had introduced the word and he spoke of the world. One of Freire's books is subtitled *Reading the Word and the World.* Yet Floyd was not likely to move those who were not already predisposed to his worldview. His method of persuasion would obstruct such a move. His method was explicitly propaganda. He said so. Floyd would impart what he knew. Although Freire in the field would also impart, Freire the theorist would not. "In the liberating moment," he writes, "we must try to convince the students and on the other hand we must respect them, not impose ideas on them" (Shor and Freire 33, 46). For all that was valid—even necessary—in what Floyd had said, there was no dialectic in his class.

So myths prevailed, for the most part. Those students who saw the hope of African American peoples in religion wrote of salvation through prayer and devotion, of future good in suffering now. Those who followed the tenets of nonviolent protest, wrote of the steady progress African Americans have known since the struggles of Martin Luther King. Those who believed in simple, undirected opposition wrote of "blue-eyed devils." The students had not been politically affected in the manner Floyd had apparently intended.

Freire notes that one who is not of the mainstream is "[i]rresistibly attracted by the life style of the director society, alienated man is a nostalgic man, never truly committed to his world" (*Cultural Action* 2). Although Freire seems to censure this alienated man, I believe that the American of color is predisposed to this kind of alienation. Victims of oppression tend to be enamored of their oppressors. Consider the great numbers of minorities who make careers in the military service, for example. This cannot be accounted for solely on the basis of economic security. We would have our Americanism recognized and acknowledged. Oppressor and oppressed have histories, cultures, ideologies, traditions in common. We are us, and we are them.

Floyd's students were in the Writer's Project because they held some traditional national-cultural beliefs. They were in school to fulfill a dream, a longtime American dream of success through education. They were not in school to have their dreams destroyed. They would naturally resist any such attempt. Floyd's students could reason that no matter how slight their chances of getting into college or the middle class, they did have chances, maybe better than most. After all, Floyd had said that they were special, that they were leaders, world-changers. Floyd had himself made it through college, was a teacher, a published poet, a world traveler to pan-African conferences. In the students' eyes Floyd made a better model of the bootstrap mentality than of the revolutionary one. They said so: "He's bad. You know. He got no-tay-rye-eh-tee. I mean with the bad rags and the ride and like that."

It is not as if the students had no collective sense, did not see class difference and race. As Signithia Fordham observes, African American youths who wish to succeed in school simply have no reason to assume that collectivity is a necessary precondition for such success. Individuals have gone further than the race. All castelike minorities have their successful individuals—big stars, successful businessmen, prominent politicians. The impetus for a radical collective is not readily apparent.

How could a collectivity gathered for revolution be appealing to adolescents seeking access, after all? Floyd might have seen revolution as consciousness raising, as the demystification of otherwise mysterious class and cultural forces, but the word "revolution" nevertheless conjures up frightening pictures: not acts of criticism, but acts of violence, undertaken when there is nothing left to lose. Yet there are things left to lose here. There might still be pie. Enough African Americans get through at least the class system to prove that there are still gains to be had. As far as Floyd's students could see—as far as American society, in general, is concerned—conditions for African Americans and others of color are getting better. More of those who have been traditionally excluded are gaining access.

But the basic inequities remain. Reyes and Halcón report, drawing from Census Bureau figures, that there are just over 7,000 Latinos who hold Ph.D.s in America, up from an estimate in 1970 of less than a

100 (though this last estimate was restricted to Chicanos). This is an impressive increase. Yet Reyes and Halcón also note that Latinos comprise only 2.1 percent of all American doctorates. Numbers go up; percentages still tell of the need for radical change. Still, the numbers do go up. And the numbers do give hope. Hope undermines Floyd's zeal, negates Floyd's call to arms. One successful figure—Floyd—extolling the students' abilities for success, is not likely to persuade those students that a revolutionary consciousness is a better definition of success than individual fame or fortune.

There really was something wonderful in what Floyd was attempting. If it had been more successful there would have been the beginnings of an America living up to its ideals, a chance for anyone, no matter the birth ascription, to take part in all the country has to offer. But Floyd had missed an important ideological concern—the power of the ideology of individualism in our country. A collective sense, a larger global sense of what happens to individuals who are too often seen as members of a particular group, must come from within. It's at the core of Freire's philosophy. Floyd had the right sensibility, perhaps, but the wrong method. Authoritarianism is authoritarianism, no matter what the authority is espousing. To dictate is not to liberate. The message is too much the contradiction: "You will be free if you do as I say." The message is too easily resisted if the primary human will is, as Freire asserts, toward realizing freedom.

Sgt. V enjoyed listening to Bracy and the men from Palo Alto. They made sense to him. But it seemed to him that their kind of education was a luxury. Sgt. V was already on a career path, with a wife and with a baby on the way, still holding hopes for his piece of the pie.

Three months after his reenlistment, he receives orders for an unaccompanied tour of duty in Korea. He's allowed to remain in California long enough to see his son enter the world. Two months later he's in ASCOM depot, Korea.

Vietnam was war. One accepts war as absurd, beyond notions of reality; one goes through the motions without much thought, not even thoughts of the absurdity, only of death and staying alive and returning to the world and maybe the block. The things one has done to stay alive, the morality involved, the rationalizations tendered to account for war at all, those thoughts come later, again and again, as one grows older. But not then, not in the boy's mind set on survival. Wars are fought by boys. An older boy, more a man, enters Korea, and the absurdities are bare. Korea was not war.

In college I would read Camus. I would also read *La Cantatrise Chauve* and other plays of the Theater of the Absurd, the philosophy of existentialism. I would enjoy them and know not to try to make rational sense of them, that that was the point. Some things are absurd, beyond logic in the living. I could appreciate the absurd, I think, because of Korea. And I could begin to appreciate that individual lives can be directed by unseen forces, absurdities.

Korea: a theater of the absurd.

Walking through Seoul: school kids. Girls in uniform, much like girls in American parochial schools, pleated, plaid jumpers with white blouses and ties. All the Korean girls have long, black hair in braids— except one. She has short hair. It is explained that hair is worn long until a certain age or until virginity is lost. The girl with the short hair is probably Eurasian, comes the explanation, even if she doesn't look it. An original sin. The boys wear fatigues, are performing military drills with wooden rifles. This is PE. War is assumed.

A young man in his teens is seated in the middle of a busy intersection. A policeman in uniform, white policeman's hat, white gloves, is applying old-fashioned barber's shears, an older version of the electric ones used by barbers to trim napes of necks. A public haircut. Only men in the entertainment industry are allowed long hair. Legislated conformity.

A bus filled with American GIs is halted along an otherwise deserted road, waiting for a train to go by. In the field alongside, a squad of ROK, Republic of Korea Army soldiers. They are double-timing in unison. Suddenly they veer off, still in unison, coming directly for the bus. They line up, one squad on its knees, one squad kneeling on the first, the other two squads standing between, all but the bottom row with hands on the bus. They rock the bus, while inside the GIs are yelling to the ROKs. The ROKs push the bus over on its side, shout like a home run had just been hit, regroup, continue double-timing away. GIs have to climb out windows.

A restaurant in Yongsan, Seoul, white tablecloths, fine crystal and china, every individual seated at the table has an individual waiter standing at attention, eyes straight ahead, tuxedo pants, white shirt, tuxedo vest, white linen folded over a forearm, filling glasses of water after every sip. The sergeant feels some discomfort at this excess of service, makes a comment, is told by his individual waiter, "The sky the rimit." Not for the waiter, apparently.

The military compound contains a golf course and country club which divides the quarters for military who are unaccompanied, without family, and the family quarters. Family quarters look like Anytown, USA: individual houses with driveways, a typical American suburban grade school with a push-type carousel, wide streets, cul-de-sacs. At the commissary, American women in stylish clothes leave their cars, escorted by Korean men in chauffeur's uniforms, the men holding parasols over the women's heads. The chauffeurs scurry back to the cars to wipe the cars with large feathered dust mops. Outside the compound, the big chevys and oldsmobiles can hardly make it through the narrow, chuckholed streets. Directly outside the compound are wooden shanties housing strings of bars which double as whorehouses.

The unaccompanied military have houseboys: men who wash, starch and press the GIs' clothes, spit shine their boots and shoes, clean their living areas, prepare their lockers and barracks for inspections, all for five dollars a month per GI. One of the houseboys is Mr. Yi, a man in his thirties, married, two children, a college student who speaks Japanese, French, and English. He notices the sergeant spends his time reading. They begin to have conversations. The houseboy tells him that many students, maybe most, do not care for America's military presence and resent that the presidents of their largest corporations, Shinjun Auto and Korean Air Lines, are headed by retired American military, that they would rather have a reunification of North and South without the political influences of either the Communist Chinese or the Americans, that they believe the reason the Korean government puts up with the old-fashioned colonialism of American military presence is because the presence is a condition of neo-colonialism, that the government is under an unavoidable American economic influence. He explains colonial theory, tells the sergeant about American history, how after the Second World War America became a worldwide imperial power, says that American people are good but politically naive. The sergeant tells of the preservation of democracy, the reason he's been told that he is there, how America just wants everyone to enjoy the freedoms it has. The houseboy says there is no Korean democracy, not even the representative democracy of America, not really.

Korean President Pak Chun Hi declares martial law, trains tanks on his own citizenry, announces that the military will relax when the people vote for a change in the Constitution that will allow him another term as president. American GIs, there to protect democracy, continue business as usual, are not even put on alert.

Sgt. V returns home shortly thereafter. He arrives to find no one seems to know about President Pak's martial law. A Saturday morning, watching cartoons with his son, he sees *In the News,* a five-minute news blurb aimed at children. It is there that the Korean situation is mentioned. He begins to wonder how such big events could be so effectively kept from so many. A flood of memories, a rising consciousness, a critical consciousness.

V *Inglés* in the Colleges

It was said to be the oldest apartment house in the city of Seattle: from nineteenth-century loggers' quarters to whorehouse to tenement. It stood on a hill at the gateway to the south side. Nights would be filled with the sounds of foghorns coming in from the Puget Sound and the sounds of gunfire from within the neighborhood.

There were other sounds as well. There was the whirring of a sewing machine long into the night: the Vietnamese family doing piecework for a company that made baseball caps. There were the clucks of chickens or honks of geese from the Cambodian family, the crack of a rock when fowl were slaughtered for food. The whoops of joy from the Nigerian fellow the day he was served with deportation papers (couldn't have afforded to return to his home otherwise). The screams of anguish from the panhandler a few doors down the day the government worker took her children away. The long talks about Latin American coffee from the retired merchant marine with the game leg. There was the occasional shout through the kitchen window: "If you can't beat 'em, join 'em." Angry talk about American academics from the apartment manager: a man from India who had recently gotten his Ph.D. in history from the prestigious university but couldn't land a job. There were the family sounds: children at play; the clickings of a 1941 Remington typewriter long enough into the night to know of the whirring sewing machine next door; the nightly screeching and scratching of rats crawling within the walls; the crunching on cockroach carcasses the day the exterminator came by. These were the sounds that came from and came to the one-bedroom apartment of Victor and Carol and their children. And there was the friendly chatter when all gathered by the mailboxes on the eighth of each month, anticipating the mailman and food stamps, discussing different versions of what that great meal would be that night, enjoying a few days' balm after long sorenesses.

Summer mornings, Carol would walk down to the free-bus zone to get to her job in telemarketing, bothering people in their homes for minimum wage. Victor would go with his daughter to the food bank on Empire Way—mainstreet in the heart of the ghetto, the location of the Welfare office, the empire's way—then to the food bank at the Freemont District, then the food bank at the local Catholic Church. Some bags would contain frozen juices or frozen burritos or frozen turnovers, but the apartment had no working freezer and no working oven. Miles for meals. Carol would return, and Victor would walk the five miles to the University to teach his basic-writing class. Pride at teaching; humiliation at food-bank lines, free government cheese and butter lines, welfare lines. He had known greater affluence as a sergeant in the Army. Dr. V, the college professor, can still make that claim, the difference between then and now, matters of degree rather than kind. But he had made a choice, had opted out of the army.

The morality of war, the morality of military occupation, the morality of forced separation from family, all had become unignorable. Memories of Dad speaking about the Americans who would be in charge of the virtually all Puerto Rican American forces in Puerto Rico, of the resentment Dad heard about from the Panamanians when he had served as an American soldier in Panama; Dad's discharge papers reading "WPR," White Puerto Rican; Dad's dissertations on the large American corporations' profiting by being located in Puerto Rico but not passing on the profits to the majority of Puerto Ricans on the Island—all such memories had come flooding back as he thought of his experiences in the Army, especially in Korea, the similarities unignorable. And there were the officers the sergeant from *el bloque* had served under, particularly those whose sole qualification for leadership seemed to be their college degrees, those who seemed no brighter than he, no more competent. And there was Walter Myles, a peer, from the block, even if in Palo Alto; Walter, of color—and a college graduate. It was time to move on, away from the Army.

I wanted to try my hand at college, go beyond the GED. But college scared me. I had been told long ago that college wasn't my lot.

He drives by the University District of Seattle during his last days in the military and sees the college kids, long hair and sandals, baggy short pants on the men, long, flowing dresses on the women, some men in suits, some women in high heels, all carrying backpacks over one shoulder. There is both purpose and contentment in the air. Storefronts carry names like Dr. Feelgood and Magus Bookstore, reflecting the good feelings and magic he senses. A block away is the University, red tiles and green grass, rolling hills and tall pines, apple and cherry blossoms, the trees shading modern monoliths of gray concrete and gothic, church-like buildings of red brick. And he says to himself, "Maybe in the next life."

He must be content with escaping a life at menial labor, at being able to bank on the skills in personnel management he had acquired in the Army. But there are only two takers. The large department-store chain would hire him as a management trainee—a shoe salesman on commission, no set income, but a trainee could qualify for GI Bill benefits as well as the commissions. Not good enough, not getting paid beyond the GI Bill; and a sales career wasn't good enough either, the thought of his mother's years as a saleslady, years lost, still in memory. A finance corporation offers him a job: management trainee. The title: Assistant Manager. The job: bill collector, with low wage, but as a trainee, qualified to supplement with the GI Bill. The combined pay would be good, but he would surely lose his job in time, would be unable to be righteously indignant like the bill collectors he has too often had to face too often are, unable to bother people like Mom and Dad, knowing that being unable to meet bills isn't usually a moral shortcoming but most often an economic condition.

The GI Bill had come up again, however, setting the "gettinover" wheels in motion. The nearby community college charges ninety dollars a quarter tuition, would accept him on the strength of his GED scores. That would mean nearly four hundred dollars a month from the GI Bill, with only thirty dollars a month for schooling ("forgetting" to account for books and supplies). What a get-over! There would be immediate profit in simply going to school. And if he failed, there would be nothing lost. And if he succeeded, an Associate degree in something. He'd be better equipped to brave the job market again.

So he walks onto the community college campus in the summer of 1976. It's not the campus of the University of Washington. It's more like Dominguez High School in California. But it is a college. Chemistry: a clumsiness at the lab, but relative grace at mathematical equations and memorization. French is listening to audiotapes and filling out workbooks. History is enjoyable stories, local lore from a retired newsman, easy memorization for the grade.

Then there is English. There are the stories, the taste he had always had for reading, now peppered with talk of philosophy and psychology and tensions and textures. Writing is 200 words on anything, preceded by a sentence outline. He'd write about Korea and why *The Rolling Stone* could write about conspiracies of silence, or he'd write about the problems in trying to get a son to understand that he is Puerto Rican when the only Puerto Ricans he knows are his grandparents; he'd write about whatever seemed to be on his mind at the time. The night before a paper would be due, he'd gather pen and pad, and stare. Clean the dishes. Stare. Watch an "I Love Lucy" rerun. Stare. Then sometime in the night the words would come. He'd write; scratch something out; draw arrows shifting paragraphs around; add a phrase or two. Then he'd pull out the erasable bond, making changes even as he typed, frantic to be done before school. Then he'd use the completed essay to type out an outline, feeling a little guilty about having cheated in not having produced the outline first.

The guilt showed one day when Mrs. Ray, the Indian woman in traditional dress with a Ph.D. in English from Oxford, part-time instructor at the community college, said there was a problem with his writing. She must have been able to tell somehow that he was discovering what to write while writing, no prior thesis statement, no outline, just a vague notion that would materialize, magically, while writing. In her stark, small office she hands him a sheet with three familiar sayings mimeoed on it; instructs him to write on one, right there, right then. He writes on "a bird in the hand is worth two in the bush." No memory of what he had written, probably forgotten during the writing. Thirty minutes or so later, she takes the four or five pages he had written; she reads; she smiles; then she explains that she had suspected plagiarism in his previous writings. She apologizes, saying she found his writing "too serious," too abstract, not typical of her students. He is not insulted; he is flattered. He knew he could read; now he knew he could write well enough for college.

English 102, Mr. Lukens devotes a portion of the quarter to Afro-American literature. Victor reads Ishmael Reed, "I'm a Cowboy in the Boat of Ra." It begins,

> I am a cowboy in the boat of Ra,
> sidewinders in the saloons of fools
> bit my forehead like   O
> the untrustworthiness of Egyptologists
> Who do not know their trips. Who was that
> dog faced man? they asked, the day I rode
> from town.
>
> School marms with halitosis cannot see
> the Nefertitti fake chipped on the run by slick
> germans, the hawk behind Sonny Rollins' head or
> the ritual beard of his axe; a longhorn winding
> its bells thru the Field of Reeds.

There was more, but by this point he was already entranced and excited. Poetry has meaning, more than the drama of Mark Antony's speech years back.

Mr. Lukens says that here is an instance of poetry more for effect (or maybe *affect*) than for meaning, citing a line from Archibald

MacLeish: "A poem should not mean / But be." But there *was* meaning in this poem. Victor writes about it. In the second stanza, the chipped Nefertitti, a reference to a false black history, with images from "The Maltese Falcon" and war movies. The "School marms" Reed mentions are like the schoolmasters at Hamilton, unknowing and seeming not to know of being unknowing. Sonny Rollins' axe and the Field of Reeds: a saxophone, a reed instrument, the African American's links to Egypt, a history whitewashed by "Egyptologists / Who do not know their trips." He understood the allusions, appreciated the wordplay. The poem had the politics of Bracy, the language of the block, TV of the fifties, together in the medium Mr. D had introduced to Victor, Papi, but now more powerful. This was fun; this was politics. This was Victor's history, his life with language play.

Years later, Victor is on a special two-man panel at a conference of the Modern Language Association. He shares the podium with Ishmael Reed. Victor gives a talk on "Teaching as Social Action," receives applause, turns to see Ishmael Reed looking him in the eye, applauding loudly. He tries to convey how instrumental this "colleague" had been in his life.

He'll be an English major. Mr. Lukens is his advisor, sets up the community college curriculum in such a way as to have all but the major's requirements for a BA from the University of Washington out of the way. The University of Washington is the only choice: it's relatively nearby, tuition for Vietnam veterans is $176 a quarter. "Maybe in this life."

His AA degree in his back pocket, his heart beating audibly with exhilaration and fear, he walks up the campus of the University of Washington, more excited than at Disneyland when he was sixteen. He's proud: a regular transfer student, no special minority waivers. The summer of 1977.

But the community is not college in the same way the University is. The community college is torn between vocational training and preparing the unprepared for traditional university work. And it seems unable to resolve the conflict (see Cohen and Brawer). His high community-college GPA is no measure of what he is prepared to undertake at the University. He fails at French 103, unable to carry the French conversations, unable to do the reading, unable to do the writing, dropping the course before the failure becomes a matter of record. He starts again. French 101, only to find he is still not really competitive with the white kids who had had high school French. But he cannot fail, and he does not fail, thanks to hour after hour with French tapes after his son's in bed.

English 301, the literature survey, is fun. Chaucer is a ghetto boy, poking fun at folks, the rhyming reminding him of when he did the dozens on the block; Chaucer telling bawdy jokes: "And at the wyndow out she putte hir hole . . . 'A berd, a berd!,' quod hende Nicholas." So this is literature. Chaucer surely ain't white. At least he doesn't sound white, "the first to write poetry in the vernacular," he's told. Spenser is exciting: images of knights and damsels distressing, magic and dragons, the *Lord of the Rings* that he had read in Korea paling in the comparison. Donne is a kick: trying to get laid when he's Jack Donne, with a rap the boys from the block could never imagine; building church floors with words on a page when he's Dr. John Donne. Every reading is an adventure, never a nod, no matter how late into the night the reading. For his first paper, Victor, the 3.8 at Tacoma Community College, gets 36 out of a possible 100—"for your imagination," written alongside the grade.

I was both devastated and determined, my not belonging was verified but I was not ready to be shut down, not so quickly. So to the library to look up what the Professor himself had published: *Proceedings of the Spenser Society.* I had no idea what the Professor was going on about in his paper, but I could see the pattern: an introduction that said something about what others had said, what he was going to be writing about, in what order, and what all this would prove; details about what he said he was going to be writing about, complete with quotes, mainly from the poetry, not much from other writers on Spenser; and a "therefore." It wasn't the five-paragraph paper Mr. Lukens had insisted on, not just three points, not just repetition of the opening in the close, but the pattern was essentially the same. The next paper: 62 out of 100 and a "Much better." Course grade: B. Charity.

I never vindicated myself with that professor. I did try, tried to show that I didn't need academic charity. Economic charity was hard enough. I took my first graduate course from him. This time I got an "All well and good, but what's the point?" alongside a "B" for a paper. I had worked on that paper all summer long.

I have had to face that same professor, now a Director of Freshman Writing, at conferences. And with every contact, feelings of insecurity well up from within, the feeling that I'm seen as the minority (a literal term in academics for those of us of color), the feeling of being perceived as having gotten through *because* I am a minority, an insecurity I face often. But though I never got over the stigma with that professor (whether real or imagined), I did get some idea on how to write for the University.

Professorial Discourse Analysis became a standard practice: go to the library; see what the course's professor had published; try to discern a pattern to her writing; try to mimic the pattern. Some would begin with anecdotes. Some would have no personal pronouns. Some would cite others' research. Some would cite different literary works to make assertions about one literary work. Whatever they did, I would do too. And it worked, for the most part, so that I could continue the joy of time travel and mind travel with those, and within those, who wrote about things I had discovered I liked to think about: Shakespeare and work versus pleasure, religion and the day-to-day world, racism, black Othello and the Jewish Merchant of Venice; Dickens and the impossibility of really getting into the middle class (which I read as "race," getting into the white world, at the time), pokes at white folks (though the Podsnaps were more likely jabs at the middle class); Milton and social responsibility versus religious mandates; Yeats and being assimilated and yet other (critically conscious with a cultural literacy, I'd say now); others and other themes. And soon I was writing like I had written in the community college: some secondary reading beforehand, but composing the night before a paper was due, a combination of fear that nothing will come and faith that something would eventually develop, then revising to fit the pattern discovered in the Professorial Discourse Analysis, getting "A's" and "B's," and getting comments like "I never saw that before."

There were failures, of course. One professor said my writing was too formulaic. One professor said it was too novel. Another wrote only one word for the one paper required of the course: "nonsense." But while I was on the campus I could escape and not. I could think about the things that troubled me or intrigued me, but through others' eyes in other times and other places. I couldn't get enough, despite the pain and the insecurity.

School becomes his obsession. There is the education. But the obsession is as much, if not more, in getting a degree, not with a job in mind, just the degree, just because he thinks he can, despite all that has said he could not. His marriage withers away, not with rancor, just melting into a dew. The daily routine has him taking the kid to a day-care/school at 6:00 a.m., then himself to school, from school to work as a groundskeeper for a large apartment complex; later, a maintenance man, then a garbage man, then a plumber, sometimes coupled with other jobs: shipping clerk for the library, test proctor. From work to pick up the kid from school, prepare dinner, maybe watch a TV show with the kid, tuck him into bed, read. There are some girlfriends along the way, and he studies them too: the English major who won constant approval from the same professor who had given him the 36 for being imaginative; the art major who had traveled to France (French practice); the fisheries major whose father was an executive vice president for IBM (practice at being middle class). Victor was going to learn—quite consciously—what it means to be white, middle class. He didn't see the exploitation; not then; he was obsessed. There were things going on in his classes that he did not understand and that the others did. He didn't know what the things were that he didn't understand, but he knew that even those who didn't do as well as he did, somehow did not act as foreign as he felt. He was the only colored kid in every one of those classes. And he hadn't the time nor the racial affiliation to join the Black Student Union or Mecha. He was on his own, an individual pulling on his bootstraps, looking out for number one. He's not proud of the sensibility, but isolation—and, likely, exploitation of others—are the stuff of racelessness.

There were two male friends, Mickey, a friend to this day, and Luis el Loco. Luis was a *puertoriceño,* from Puerto Rico, who had found his way to Washington by having been imprisoned in the federal penitentiary at MacNeal Island, attending school on a prison-release program. Together, they would enjoy talking in Spanglish, listening to *salsa.* But Luis was a Modern Languages major, Spanish literature. Nothing there to exploit. It's a short-lived friendship. Mickey was the other older student in Victor's French 101 course, white, middle class, yet somehow other, one who had left the country during Vietnam, a disc jockey in Amsterdam. The friendship begins with simply being the two older men in the class, longer away from adolescence than the rest; the friendship grows with conversations about politics, perceptions about America from abroad, literature. But Victor would not be honest with his friend about feeling foreign until years later, a literary bravado. Mickey was well read in the literary figures Victor was coming to know. Mickey would be a testing ground for how Victor was reading, another contact to be exploited. Eventually, Mickey and his wife would introduce Victor to their friend, a co-worker at the post office. This is Carol. She comes from a life of affluence, and from a life of poverty, a traveler within the class system, not a journey anyone would volunteer for, but one which provides a unique education, a path not unlike Paulo Freire's. From her, there is the physical and the things he would know of the middle class, discussed explicitly, and there is their mutual isolation. There is love and friendship, still his closest friend, still his lover.

But before Carol, there is simply the outsider obsessed. He manages the BA. He cannot stop, even as the GI Bill reaches its end. He will continue to gather credentials until he is kicked out. Takes the GRE, does not do well, but gets into the graduate program with the help of references from within the faculty—and with the help of minority status in a program decidedly low in numbers of minorities. "Minority," or something like that, is typed on the GRE test results in his file, to be seen while scanning the file for the references. His pride is hurt, but he remembers All Saints, begins to believe in the biases of standardized tests: back in the eighth grade, a failure top student; now a near-failure, despite a 3.67 at the competitive Big University of State. Not all his grades, he knew, were matters of charity. He had earned his GPA, for the most part. Nevertheless, he is shaken.

More insecure than ever, there are no more overnight papers. Papers are written over days, weeks, paragraphs literally cut and laid out on the floor to be pasted. One comment appears in paper after paper: "Logic?" He thinks, "Yes." He does not understand. Carol cannot explain the problem. Neither can Mickey. He does not even consider asking the professors. To ask would be an admission of ignorance, "stupid spic" still resounding within. This is his problem.

Then by chance (exactly how is now forgotten), he hears a tape of a conference paper delivered by the applied linguist Robert Kaplan. Kaplan describes contrastive rhetoric. Kaplan describes a research study conducted in New York City among Puerto Ricans who are bilingual and Puerto Ricans who are monolingual in English, and he says that the discourse patterns, the rhetorical patterns which include the logic, of monolingual Puerto Ricans are like those of Puerto Rican bilinguals and different from Whites, more Greek than the Latin-like prose of American written English. Discourse analysis takes on a new intensity. At this point, what this means is that he will have to go beyond patterns in his writing, become more analytical of the connections between ideas. The implications of Kaplan's talk, for him at least, will take on historical and political significance as he learns more of rhetoric.

About the same time as that now lost tape on Kaplan's New York research (a study that was never published, evidently), Victor stumbles into his first rhetoric course.

The preview of course offerings announces a course titled "Theories of Invention," to be taught by Anne Ruggles Gere. His GRE had made it clear that he was deficient in Early American Literature. Somewhere in his mind he recalls reading that Benjamin Franklin had identified himself as an inventor; so somehow, Victor interprets "Theories of Invention" as "Theories of Inventors," an American lit course. What he discovers is Rhetoric.

Not all at once, not just in that first class on rhetoric, I discover some things about writing, my own, and about the teaching of writing. I find some of modern composition's insights are modern hindsights. I don't mind the repetition. Some things bear repeating. The repetitions take on new significance and are elaborated upon in a new context, a new time. Besides, not everyone who teaches writing knows of rhetoric, though I believe everyone should.

I read Cicero's *de Inventione*. It's a major influence in rhetoric for centuries. The strategies he describes on how to argue a court case bears a remarkable resemblance to current academic discourse, the pattern I first discovered when I first tried to figure out what I had not done in that first English course at the University.

Janet Emig looks to depth psychology and studies on creativity and even neurophysiology, the workings of the brain's two hemispheres, to pose the case that writing is a mode of learning. She explains what I had been doing with my first attempts at college writing, neither magic nor a perversion. Cicero had said much the same in his *de Oratore* in the first century BCE (Before the Common Era, the modern way of saying BC):

> *Writing* is said to be *the best and most excellent modeler and teacher of oratory;* and not without reason; for if what is meditated and considered easily surpasses sudden and extemporary speech, a constant and diligent habit of writing will surely be of more effect than meditation and consideration itself; since all the arguments relating to the subject on which we write, whether they are suggested by art, or by a certain power of genius and under-standing, will present themselves, and occur to us, while we examine and contemplate it in the full light of our intellect and all the thoughts and words, which are the most expressive of their kind, must of necessity come under and submit to the keenness of our judgment while writing; and a fair arrangement and collocation of the words is effected by writing, in a certain rhythm and measure, not poetical, but oratorical. (*de Oratore* I.cxxxiv)

Writing is a way of discovering, of learning, of thinking. Cicero is arguing the case for literacy in ways we still argue or are arguing anew.

David Bartholomae and Anthony Petrosky discuss literary theorists like Jonathan Culler and the pedagogical theorist Paulo Freire to come up with a curriculum in which reading is used to introduce basic writers, those students who come into the colleges not quite prepared for college work, to the ways of academic discourse. Quintilian, like others of his time, the first century CE, and like others before his time, advocates reading as a way to come to discover the ways of language and the ways of writing and the ways to broaden the range of experience.

Kenneth Bruffee, Peter Elbow, and others, see the hope of democratizing the classroom through peer-group learning. So did Quintilian:

> But as emulation is of use to those who have made some advancement of learning, so, to those who are but beginning and still of tender age, to imitate their schoolfellows is more pleasant than to imitate their master, for the very reason that it is more easy; for they who are learning the first rudiments will scarcely dare to exalt themselves to the hope of attaining that eloquence which they regard as the highest; they will rather fix on what is nearest to them, as vines attached to trees fain the top by taking hold of the lower branches first (23–24).

Quintilian describes commenting on student papers in ways we consider new:

> [T]he powers of boys sometimes sink under too great severity in correction; for they despond, and grieve, and at last hate their work; and what is most prejudicial, while they fear everything; they cease to attempt anything. . . . A teacher ought, therefore, to be as agreeable as possible, that remedies, which are rough in their nature, may be rendered soothing by gentleness of hand; he ought to praise some parts of his pupils' performances, tolerate some, and to alter others, giving his reasons why the alterations are made. (100)

Richard Haswell recommends minimal scoring of student papers, sticking to one or two items in need of correction per paper. Nancy Sommers warns against rubber-stamp comments on student papers, comments like "awk"; she says comments ought to explain. Both have more to say than Quintilian on such matters, but in essence both are Quintilian revisited.

Edward P. J. Corbett looks to Quintilian, Cicero, and others from among the ancients, especially Aristotle, to write *Classical Rhetoric for the Modern Student*. In some ways, the book says little that is different from other books on student writing. But the book is special in its explicit connections to ancient rhetorical traditions.

Without a knowledge of history and traditions, we risk running in circles while seeking new paths. Without knowing the traditions, there is no way of knowing which traditions to hold dear and which to discard. Self evident? Maybe. Yet the circles exist.

For all the wonders I had found in literature—and still find—literature seemed to me self-enveloping. What I would do is read and enjoy. And, when it was time to write, what I would write about would be an explanation of what I had enjoyed, using words like *Oedipal complex* or *polyvocal* or *anxiety* or *unpacking,* depending on what I had found in my discourse-analytical journeys, but essentially saying "this is what I saw" or "this is how what I read took on a special meaning for me" (sometimes being told that what I had seen or experienced was nonsense). I could imagine teaching literature—and often I do, within the context of composition—but I knew that at best I'd be imparting or imposing one view: the what I saw or the meaning for me. The reader-response theorists I would come to read, Rosenblatt, Fish, Culler, and others, would make sense to me, that what matters most is what the reader finds. Bakhtin's cultural and political dimension would make even more sense: that all language is an approximation, generated and understood based on what one has experienced with language. In teaching literature, I thought, there would be those among students I would face who would come to take on reading, perhaps; likely some who would appreciate more fully what they had read. But it did not seem to me that I could somehow make someone enjoy. Enjoyment would be a personal matter: from the self, for the self.

And what if I did manage a Ph.D. and did get a job as a professor? I would have to publish. A guest lecturer in a medieval lit course spoke of one of the important findings in his new book: medieval scribes were conscious of the thickness of the lozenge, the medieval version of the comma. He found that thinner lozenges would indicate a slight pause in reading; thicker lozenges, longer pauses. Interesting, I reckon. Surely of interest to a select few. But so what, in some larger sense? What would I write about?

Then I stumbled onto rhetoric. Here was all that language had been to me. There were the practical matters of writing and teaching writing. There were the stylistic devices, the tricks of language use that most people think about when they hear the word *rhetoric;* "Let's cut through the rhetoric." It's nice to have those devices at one's disposal—nice, even important, to know when those devices are operating. But there is more. Rhetoric's classic definition as the art of persuasion suggests a power. So much of what we do when we speak or write is suasive in intent. So much of what we receive from others—from family and friends to thirty-second blurbs on TV—is intended to persuade. Recognizing how this is done gives greater power to choose. But rhetoric is still more.

Rhetoric is the conscious use of language: "observing in any given case the available means of persuasion," to quote Aristotle (I.ii). As the conscious use of language, rhetoric would include everything that is conveyed through language: philosophy, history, anthropology, psychology, sociology, literature, politics—"the use of language as a symbolic means of inducing cooperation in beings that by nature respond to symbols," according to modern rhetorician Kenneth Burke (46). The definition says something about an essentially human characteristic: our predilection to use symbols. Language is our primary symbol system. The ability to learn language is biologically transmitted. Burke's definition points to language as ontological, part of our being. And his definition suggests that it is epistemological, part of our thinking, an idea others say more about (see Leff).

So to study rhetoric becomes a way of studying humans. Rhetoric becomes for me the complete study of language, the study of the ways in which peoples have accomplished all that has been accomplished beyond the instinctual. There were the ancient greats saying that there was political import to the use of language. There were the modern greats saying that how one comes to know is at least mediated by language, maybe even constituted in language. There were the pragmatic applications. There was the possibility that in teaching writing and in teaching rhetoric as conscious considerations of language use I could help others like myself: players with language, victims of the language of failure.

In rhetoric, there is history and culture and language with political and personal implications. From Plato I could speculate on why, perhaps, plurality receives so much resistance in our society, even when it is espoused. Plato saw a plurality of the senses as somehow base, good only insofar as the senses could lead to the supersensible, to the one unifying principle of another plane of existence, the ideal, the Idea of the Good. In his *Republic* he argues the case for censorship, in the name of the moral good of young minds. And I know that this continues, despite freedoms of the press. He argues against democracy, as a kind of government that would have everyone running after sensual self-interest, a kind of anarchy. And I think of James Madison's *Federalist Paper #10,* arguing against what he terms "pure democracy" when trying to get the Constitution ratified in New York. Plato was an influence on Cicero; Cicero was an influence on the Founding Fathers (Hirsch, *Cultural Literacy* 109).

In Plato's works on rhetoric, he lambasts the group of rhetoricians known as the sophists for speaking in pluralistic terms, reducing, in *Gorgias,* the sophists to those who simply make the worse case appear the better. There was more to the sophists, as I'll outline below. Plato's ideal rhetoric becomes one that deals in abstractions, the supersensible, a use of language to liberate the mind. And I think of *e pluribus unum,* and how the emphasis seems to be on the *unum,* as in current attempts at English Only legislation, as in the 100 percent Americanism propaganda campaigns earlier this century. "From many, one" is pretty abstract, able to be interpreted as a phrase of conformity or one of pluralism. I think of the guarantees that are not granted by the Constitution, as great as that document may be, the lack of the sensorial, the physical, the lack of guarantees to the right to live, in a very basic sense; no guarantees of health or hearth, homelessness and hunger, in a country of affluence, dismissed through the ideology of individualism: "Well, if they'd stop being so lazy, picked themselves up by the bootstraps. . . ." And I think of teaching ideas to liberate minds, a liberal education, something divorced from education as political, from a liberatory education. Liberating lives is more concrete than liberating minds. I remember, mainly through studies in English literary history, the powerful influence of Neoplatonism, Plato adopted to Christianity in a Christian nation with a long Christian heritage, and I know that Plato is very much with us all.

Cicero demonstrates the potential political power in rhetoric. He was a major political figure in the Roman Republic, one who saw and was distressed by what he believed was a change in the government, from representative government to rule by those who held military power. His oratory was geared at preventing those changes, first through public speaking, later by speaking among the senators, and still later by political intrigue. He takes part in the plot to assassinate Julius Caesar, then Caesar's successor. His plottings are discovered; he is himself assassinated. His hands and head, the tools of the public speaker, are nailed to the Roman rostrum, the stage from which public speaking took place. There would be no more oratory of his sort: imperial Rome was coming to the fore. Rhetoric must have been seen as powerful—and dangerous.

Quintilian comes from Spain, a colony of Rome. He is educated in the language and the rhetoric of the Empire. He works for the governor of Spain; Galba, the governor, becomes Emperor of Rome. Quintilian had already become a famous lawyer, the principal occupation of orators now removed from the kinds of political power they might have enjoyed in more democratic times. He becomes a teacher of rhetoric, paid with government funds, the first chair of rhetoric, teaching rhetoric to the sons of the elite of Rome. And I see the parallels to my own new life, my life now: from the colony, teaching the language and ways of the colonizers who can afford college educations, my pay coming from the government. But more importantly, I see the power of rhetoric, no longer to be fully exercised on the rostrum, being moved to the classroom.

There are other figures from classical rhetoric who affected me, and continue to do so. But the figures just mentioned were the ones who most had me thinking in historical terms. The historical brought considerations of the cultural and the political. These particular figures, and others—the sophists, Aristotle—when placed in historical context, helped to explain what Kaplan might have been referring to when he described the rhetoric of schools as Latin and the rhetoric of New York Puerto Ricans as more Greek.

Athens, around the fifth century BCE. The sophists. They are a popular group of orators, in particular among those seeking entertainment, though unpopular in certain important circles. Among the best known, to us at least, are Protagoras and Gorgias, neither of whom is native to Athens. They are *metics,* one reason, perhaps, why they are not well liked among those special circles. *Metics,* aliens, are legislatively second class, not quite enjoying the full benefits of citizenship. Protagoras comes from Abderah, in Northern Greece, and Gorgias from Leontini, in Sicily. Though they cannot take more active parts in the politics of Athens, they serve a vital function in maintaining Athenian democracy: they train those likely to take on important roles in Athenian life, using as one of their principal themes *aretê,* rhetoric in the cause of active participation in domestic, social, and political life.

Protagoras, probably the first of the paid traveling teachers, is something of a problem in his time in that his way of seeing things poses a challenge to the dominant ideology in Athens, Ionian natural philosophy, in which things are as they are because they are in the nature of things, meant to be. Protagoras says that "man is the measure of all things." So if the human is the measure, then rulers are not specially imbued by nature to rule. If the human is the measure, then there are few natural laws; there can be equally valid truths. It was likely Protagoras who first taught that there can be opposing and, in some senses, equally valid arguments to any given case—two sides (at least) to any argument. Not only are there two sides to any argument, but anyone can be taught to present, effectively, the opposing arguments. Anyone can learn to be a rhetor, not just the select few with natural speaking abilities. Protagoras, and the sophists generally, introduced a humanistic, a subjective, ideology: humanity as ultimately responsible, able to be taught the ways in which to take on responsibility.

But a subjective and relativistic ideology could cause problems. The aristocracy could not claim a natural superiority; laws and knowledge could not claim to be absolute; everything could become subject to challenge. This relativism would find its most articulate challenge from Plato. Today, the only thing cheaper than "mere rhetoric" is "sheer sophistry," a Platonic legacy.

Democrats also had an argument against the sophists. The democrats complained that what the sophists had to offer, they could, but did not, offer to everyone. Since sophists charged fees for their services, only the wealthy were able to gain access to those services and the potential inherent in acquiring what they had to offer. The way to humanism was a commodity.

In their quest to gain customers, the sophists performed public exhibitions of their skills. These were popular, well attended. Since the public demonstrations were intended to gather students, sophistic orators were about showing off their own unique skills, not just the potential powers of rhetoric. Their speeches, then, seemed less concerned with content than with displaying artistry with language and thereby their proficiency with language.

The most popular sophist of the time was Gorgias. Among his demonstrations, one still available to us is the *Encomium to Helen,* a speech in praise of Helen. The Athenians knew the "truth" of Helen's betrayal. But Gorgias would demonstrate how he could argue skillfully that despite what the Athenians "knew" to be the case, historic Helen was not guilty of betraying Menelaus, her Attic husband, even if she did go off with the Trojan Paris. Gorgias argued that Helen was either a victim of fate, or a victim of the will of the gods, a victim of love, a victim of forcible abduction, or a victim of language. Gorgias argued that there is a kind of magic to language, stronger than individual will, that Paris might have rhetorically seduced her away in such a way that she could not have resisted.

For Gorgias, words and language are obsessions. And his demonstration reflects the attention he placed on the language. The *Helen* is replete with rhyming words and echoing rhythms, with parallelism and antithetical structures, with parallels that are even careful to contain identical numbers of syllables. This consciousness of demonstrating the rhetorical, stylistic skills of the orator, and this consciousness of the sound of the oration, even over the sense, become the marks of the sophist.

Centuries later, in the Roman Republic, Cicero is accused of being "Asiatic" in his rhetorical practices. To be Asiatic is to employ the rhetoric of Asia Minor and Greece. Its opposite, the Attic, might refer to Athens, but it is the plain, precise ways of the Latin. Cicero's writing and oratory have a flair for amplification, a stylistic device in which a certain point is repeated several times in succession, though using different words. His writing displays sophistic tendencies: parallelism, antithetical structures, amplification in order to assure a certain sound to the structure.

But because the sophists were considered morally suspect in working for money, and were surely ideologically and theologically dangerous, they were successfully squelched from Western rhetorical history (or put down) for centuries. Isocrates, a sophist, one to whom Cicero gives credit, writes *Against the Sophists;* Aristotle pits the dialectician against sophists in his *Rhetoric;* and there is Plato. Cicero himself claims not to be Asiatic because the Asiatic is philosophically empty. Yet the Ciceronian, and its sophistic ways with words, dominate Western oratorical style until the eighteenth century, when Peter Ramus redefines rhetoric in line with the new modern ways of thinking. Rhetoric is style; ideas are matters of logic. Aristotle's clarity and logic adopted to the rhetorical takes precedence over the Ciceronian (Crowley).

Then the history is gone as well as the style itself, a reference to the sophists showing up in the writing of Hegel but really only arising again during the last two decades or so.

Sophistry does arise again in the East, however. By the fourth century CE, the Roman Empire is virtually destroyed by the Visigoths, German invaders. The seat of the empire moves to Constantinople, New Rome, ruled by Constantine. This is the birth of the Byzantine Empire. By 395 CE, Christianity is adopted as the religion of the empire. Greek is the language, even though the Byzantines refer to themselves as Romans (Arnott). And the sophistic is the formal way with the language.

Philostratus calls this rebirth of florid rhetoric the Second Sophistic. Like the sophists of old, the second sophists traveled the empire giving demonstrations, celebrating the greatness of Greece and its reflection in the greatness of Rome. Maybe as early as the second century CE, the second sophistic enjoyed significant influence, even though Christians were critical because of the second sophistic's celebration of pagan mythology, and—like the old sophists—because of the second sophistic's self-indulgent attention to the speaker's skills, its emphasis on language for its own sake. But by the end of the fourth century, the second sophistic's ways were evident in the homilies and orations of Christian patristics like Gregory of Nazianzus, Basil the Great, and his brother Gregory. In 392 CE, the Byzantine Emperor Theodosius forbids pagan worship. St. John Chrysostom (John Golden-Tongued), patriarch of Constantinople, is regarded as the finest of all Christian orators in Greek, trained by the sophist Libanius (Arnott; Kennedy).

Byzantium, and thereby Byzantine rhetoric, remains relatively constant for over a thousand years, finally falling to Turkish invaders in 1453. Rome knows no such consistency, even during the Holy Roman Empire, losing to the Visigoths, retaken by Byzantium, falling to the Ostrogoths, taken and retaken for centuries. But more important for what I am presenting here, is Byzantium's relations to the Arabs and to Spain.

Byzantium had an uneasy relation with the Arabs, frequently fighting, mainly along the long border along the Caucuses and the desert, occasional attempts by Arabs at Constantinople itself. But the Byzantines and Arabs both faced a common threat from the Slavs and the Goths. So from about 395 to 636 there is an alliance between the Byzantine Empire and an Arab federation, the *foederati*. These Arabs learn enough of Constantinople's Greek ways to act as something like border mediators between Byzantium and the Arab peninsula. There are also the Rhomaic Arabs who take residence in Byzantium (Shahid). Add Byzantium's possession of Syria and Persia, later taken by the Saracens, Moslem Arabs, and there remains a relatively strong Byzantine influence to Arab rhetoric.

During these early centuries of the Byzantine Empire, the Visigoths move into Spain. There, they share the peninsula with the Suevi, another Germanic peoples. Northern Africa is taken by yet another group of Germans, the Vandals, who had settled first in southern Spain, sharing that part of the peninsula with another wandering group, the Alans. Except for the Ostrogoths in Italy, the Germanic conquerors are content to exploit, without regard to converting the native populations. We still speak of vandals as despoilers. The Byzantine Empire, however, had its sense of "Roman-ness," an historical right to rule, now joined with the Christian sense of mission. Byzantium could not allow this blow to the empire's historically proven legacy and to the empire's moral mission. By the mid-sixth century, the Byzantine Empire retakes northern Africa and southern Spain (Jenkins). A continuity from the old Roman Empire is reestablished in Spain, now more visibly bearing something of the older Greek ways. Eventually, Spain is again taken by the Visigoths, but there is nothing to suggest any attempts by the Germans to remove the Greek ways of New Rome in the ancient colony of Old Rome (Jenkins).

Mohammad enters the picture in the seventh century. Beginning in 622, Mohammad is gathering a following, having moved to Medina. It is at this time that the Byzantine emperor Heraclius is on a campaign to regain Persia for the empire, a campaign which is to succeed six years later, establishing the True Cross in Persia, the Orthodox Christianity of the Byzantines. Persia is again part of what Heraclius sees as the Roman Empire, Heraclius himself hailed as the new Scipio, Persians having to take on Christianity, the Hellenistic language of the empire, and Greco-Roman rule generally. But Orthodox Christianity had its problems, nearly two hundred years of debate over the nature or natures of Jesus. Officially, Jesus was to be regarded as having two natures, the Father and the Son. The dominant "heresy" was that Jesus had one divine nature. This was known as *monophysite.* Heraclius tries to bring the factions together, declaring in 639 that whether two natures or one, Jesus was possessed by a single energy or will. The orthodox patriarch of Jerusalem, Sophronius, condemns the idea. Pope Honarium disavows it. And Mohammad offers the Arabs, Persia, Syria, Egypt, poor and once again subject to Greco-Roman rule, an alternative, likely drawn from the Christian, the Jewish, and the Persian creeds which had been implanted in Yemen during Persian rule there: there is but one God, and Mohammad is His prophet. By 628, the same time as Heraclius's retaking of Persia, Mohammad with powerful followers, generals and caliphs, occupies Mecca, only a thousand miles south of Byzantium, formally expelling Mecca's idols. Four years later, Mohammad dies, but the wheels have been set in motion. By 639 the Saracens are in Syria and taking Egypt. Within a few decades, Islam, the "Surrender to God," is established in Persia and most of the southern and eastern parts of the New Roman Empire (Jenkins).

In 711 the Saracen Tariq ibn Ziyad, accompanied by north African Berber volunteers, sails the nine miles which divide the Pillars of Hercules and takes Spain from the Visigoth Roderic. Within the year Spain is under the control of Moslem Arabs. These are the Moors, likely getting their name in having come from Morocco. The Pillars of Hercules are eventually renamed to Jabal Musa on the African side and Jabal Tariq, Gibraltar, on the Spanish. In 732 the Saracens cross the Pyrenees, but are stopped by Charles Martel. In 756 Prince Abd-al-Rahman runs to Spain when Syria overthrows the Saracen capital. The new capital is established at Cordoba. Within 150 years Cordoba is established as the largest city in western Europe, a cultural rival to Baghdad and Constantinople. The *mezquita,* the mosque at Cordoba, remains today, displaying its Arabic calligraphy—and its Byzantine mosaics. Spain had been Byzantine and so had the Arabs. The Arabs remained (though not without conflict, like Charlemagne or the Crusades) until 1492, when Ferdinand and Isabela finally oust the Saracens, the Moors. Later in the same year Isabela commissions Christopher Columbus (Abercrombie). The Spaniard conquerors of the New World brought the Arab and the Byzantine, the sophistic, with them.

Now, I have taken this rather long-winded route because I believe it is interesting, and because a special perspective is gained in understanding the historical, as Freire and others make clear. The particular perspective gained here is that the Latino's ways with words could not help but be influenced by the 400 years in which Spain dominated so much of the New World, and that those ways would have been influenced by the 700 years of Arab domination over Spain, and by the 200 years of Byzantium, with its rhetorical heritage going back yet another 700 years. Nearly two thousand years of certain rhetorical ways, albeit in different languages, are not likely to be overcome in the hundred years and less of English domination, especially when we consider that the rhetorical history of English, though through another route, mainly Cicero, also gave a kind of sophistry special privilege up to the eighteenth century.

This gives an historical perspective to contrastive rhetoric, which has had a troubled record among linguists concerned with second language acquisition since it was first introduced by Robert Kaplan in 1966. Part of the problem with accepting the concept was Kaplan's claim in that 1966 article that different discourse patterns reflected different thought patterns, a psychological perspective that wouldn't trouble rhetoricians but would fall outside the purview of linguistics. A related problem would be that claims concerning the psychological and how rhetorical patterns might reflect different nuances of meaning would be difficult to prove empirically. Linguistics is squarely within the scientific paradigm, not given to the speculative.

But since Kaplan's first introduction, there have been empirical studies that have passed the tests of scientific rigor. These have tended to complement the historical. Shirley Ostler, comparing English and Arabic prose, found that modern Arabic prose is essentially unchanged from its Classical origins. The prose tends to have longer sentences than English prose, given to coordinate rather than to subordinate clauses. There is a tendency to balance the subject and the predicate: equal numbers of words on each side of the sentence or else a rhythmical balance. Paragraphs are longer than in English, given to long elaboration, even when there is no evidence of an attempt at being decidedly ornate. The discourse generally tends toward the global, leaning heavily on proverb-like phrases, what English would consider clichés (but what Milton or others prior to the eighteenth century would have called "commonplaces"). Another study of Arabic prose by Sa'Adeddin showed a heightened use of first- and second-person personal pronouns, indicating an attempt at close reader-writer interaction (Lux and Grabe). Ostler's research had students writing papers on personal topics, so she was not able to draw any conclusions along those lines. What she did find, however, was that the Arabic students she studied displayed features of Arabic prose in their writing in English: a greater attention to the sound of the discourse than to the sense, the language more than the logic; in short, the sophistic.

These same tendencies showed up in studies concerning the written prose of Spanish speakers. Paul Lux and William Grabe studied a large number of texts written by Ecuadorians. They found the tendency for longer sentences, greater reader-writer interaction, and a tendency among the Latin American writers to deal in the abstract. Sister Olga Santana-Seda found these same tendencies among Spanish-speaking New York Puerto Ricans, finding also that these writers tended toward non-sequential sentences, that the logical connections between sentences were not always apparent. And María Montaño-Harmon, looking at written Mexican Spanish, found the same thing, noting that the digressions were conscious, using phrases like "*Volvamos a lo que había dicho antes,*" "We'll return to what's been said later." She also found that the Spanish writers tended to what she termed hyperbole, sentences that repeated a point several times, each time using different words, each more ornate than the previous. This is a kind of amplification, the same Asiatic, sophistic tendency found in Cicero. In a side comment, Montaño-Harmon mentions that five of the Anglo-American students she studied showed rhetorical patterns more like the Spanish than the other forty-five Anglo-American writers. These five lived in a border town in southern Arizona, grew up among Chicanos, considered themselves relatively bilingual. She only makes note. But since I am not a linguist, not constrained by the empirically valid and reliable, I can speculate that these students, having come in contact with the sophistic, found it easy to take on the Spanish ways because those ways for English discourse are more deeply embedded than the less elaborated, more clearly linear, idea-centered discourse of modern English.

Nor is this idea that there is something like a linguistic memory idle speculation. Mikhail Bakhtin's theory of language as dialogic suggests something like a historical linkage to language. For Bakhtin there is no objective language "out there" waiting to be appropriated by a listener-speaker, much less a speaker-writer. We come to know the meanings in language by having heard them from others. Our own experiences add a nuance or a special turn of meaning to what we have heard, which we, in turn, pass on to others. This means that those who have passed language on to us have gathered it from others before them, each passing on the language with a newer nuance. Language, then, is social; insofar as it is social, it is also ideological, carrying various worldviews; and insofar as it is social and ideological, it is also historical. The Russian psychologist Lev Vygotsky, seeing much the same thing as Burke or Bakhtin, sees language as essentially epistemological, as the means by which we come to know, seeing the word as "a microcosm of human consciousness" (Schuster).

James McConnell suggests that memory may be biochemically transmitted through RNA (ribonucleic acid). In a series of experiments, McConnell and his associates trained a flatworm to go through a maze. The planarian was then chopped up, and the pieces were injected into other flatworms. The untrained flatworms who had received the pieces of the earlier learned to navigate the maze at a significantly faster rate than those who hadn't. Memory as physical, a body chemical biologically transmitted. Maybe. We know that language is an inherent biological quality in humans. There is at least the possibility that particular linguistic ways may be carried through RNA in something like Carl Jung's archaic imprints.

Steven, my son, was born into a monolingual household. Grandma and Grandpa spoke to him solely in English. When he first began to speak, he would say "walk-side" instead of sidewalk. No one says "walk-side." But in Spanish, nouns come before adjectives.

Steven would not get the word *toes,* a mighty simple word. He'd insist on calling toes "the fingers of the feet," a literal translation of the Spanish for toes. It was he, back then, that reminded me of the Spanish expression for toes. Where did he get this?

Whether biologically transmitted beyond the basic ability to learn language or not (to return from the flight of speculation and to skirt the possibility of being read as somehow advocating something like biological determinacy, of being an Arthur Jensen), it is clear that language is passed on by people. People would pass language on in particular ways. Those ways would reflect social and historical preferences, traditions, conventions—rhetorics.

Nor would the differences between speaking and writing, although real, alter socio-historical and culturally influenced rhetorics significantly, except consciously. At bottom, speaking and writing stem from the same source—language, the differences between speaking and writing amounting to little more than the different conventions which arise out of particular forms following particular functions, the needs for the written that can't be met by the spoken (like transmitting information to many over time, and the demands that become imposed on the language producer in not having the benefits of face-to-face interaction, as well as other things (Vachek). Both historical and empirical research suggest that for Spanish-speakers, or for those exposed to the ways of the Spanish-speaker, those preferred rhetorical ways are fundamentally sophistic.

My problems with logic in those graduate courses stemmed from my not having been exposed to a language that had as its primary focus logic. My exposure to written discourse prior to graduate school was never of the academic variety. Literature is deemed such, in part, because of the imaginative ways in which it plays with or even consciously disregards convention. Even the nonfiction I would have been exposed to in college consisted of things written when Cicero thrived, like Milton's Prolusions. When I didn't understand what was being argued in my Professorial Discourse Analyses, I did not attempt to puzzle out the logic; my concerns were with *patterns,* the sounds. I would even throw in the word *however* into my writing, without intending "on the contrary." It just sounded right. I got called on it only once, in graduate school, after three years of writing papers.

That I was able to get through undergraduate school in this way tells me that teachers have different expectations of undergraduates than of graduates. They might have been satisfied simply to see one who enjoyed playing with language, one willing to take what they perceived as chances, predisposed to being "serious," abstract, likely the only sophist in those classes, surely the only Latino, though with the fluency of the native English speaker, long ago well trained in matters of grammatical correctness and proper spelling, thereby not given the special focus of the foreign-language speaker's rhetoric by the teachers.

With graduate school, however, style must have taken a back seat to concept for many. If my writing was "too formulaic," it was likely in my using contemporary commonplaces, mimicking the formulas of psychological interpretations of texts or Harold Bloom's anxiety of influence or even deconstruction. If it was "too novel," it was likely too speculative, that global tendency of Spanish-speakers, of Arabs, of sophists; or maybe it was stylistically novel, long sentences, digressions which would prove to be relevant, but only for the patient reader. It was surely these things that prompted one professor to give me the gift for my imagination and later prompted him to ask what my point had been.

Donald Murray says "writing is revising" ("Internal Revision" 85). This is excruciatingly clear to me. If I am to discover my thinking in the writing, I must give vent to my sophistic tendencies. This is not Peter Elbow's freewriting. I agonize over word choices or sentence constructions. I deliberate over opening sentences to paragraphs, over transitions. I backtrack and redirect. I correct. But I also know that I will have to go back when I am done to reconsider the logical predispositions of my audience, make connections explicit, relegate some things to footnotes, delete others, even if they are significant to me. The more theoretical portions of this book display that consciousness. Scientific discourse is never quite in my grasp to this day, proffering drafts to those who are good at grantsmanship and the like, always receiving long "advice" on how I might revise. My writing is always subject to rhetorical "translation."

I speak of such things in courses I teach, not only for the sake of those from Latino backgrounds, but for all. There can be no telling of the linguistic backgrounds of the students. Most have not been exposed to the writing of academics. Some will—or do—teach in schools where the majority of their students will come from, or do come from, linguistic backgrounds other than English. I speak of the imperial conquests and the rhetoric that traveled with the conquerors. I introduce Averroës, the Arab Ibn Rushd, who wrote commentaries on Aristotle, and the class becomes eleventh-century Toledo (Spain, not Ohio), where Christians, Jews, and Muslims translated Averroës and thereby Aristotle into Latin.

Aristotle's ways are presented. After some talk about Aristotle's logic and rhetoric—the essential definition, induction and deduction, the syllogism, and the enthymeme, a kind of syllogism still used in argumentation—we work on the logic and language of a student's text, suggesting ways for a rhetorical translation. We test those translations by consciously seeking to use cohesive devices, words like *however* or *consequently* at the sentence level; word repetitions between sentences; transitions among paragraphs. I supply a relatively short list of such devices (see Halliday and Hasan; Markels; Witte and Faigley). We try to find cohesive devices that fit, discuss it when none does. Sometimes none should, and it's okay. Often new ways of seeing what is being attempted present themselves, re-visions. "Tighter" papers result most often, closer to revision than to correction. Ways of seeing, worldviews, and rhetorical predispositions are allowed expression; logic is not reduced to right and wrong, or even propriety; logic is explicitly discussed as yet another convention. Discussion of the historical and the rhetorical so as to be conscious of the mandates of those who rule, especially in classrooms, becomes one way to meet Freire's concern that the liberatory teacher provide a process for the development of critical consciousness without being what he terms *laissez-faire,* without denying the technical training required for academic success.

Victor the graduate student is walking to Safeway one day when one of his professors jumps out of a car to ask if he would be willing to take an academic job. The job is to be a "reader," grading papers for an undergraduate course. The requirements are that the course must have more than fifty students enrolled and that the reader be recommended by the professor teaching the course. He accepts.

Poverty has him living with his family in Mickey's unfinished, unheated basement. Victor wears his sister's down vest and his own gloves, vapor steaming from his nostrils, grading papers in line with his professor's way of seeing, not his own, all literature a reflection of archetypes, Carl Jung and Northrop Frye. Carol computes his real wages: twenty-five cents an hour. And he is grateful.

He earns a reputation as a reader, needs only to hang around the graduate student lounge the first few days of every quarter to get a job. He knows the exploitation. But it's okay somehow. One quarter he is forced to sell his *Riverside Shakespeare* for a dozen eggs, a quart of milk, and a quarter pound of coffee. He loved that book. The next quarter he is asked to be a reader for an undergraduate Shakespeare course. He receives a new copy of the *Riverside Shakespeare.* He has found a more tangible rationalization for being a reader than "good experience." The reward is the book, a symbol for the love he does not yet understand, the love of learning, the love of teaching.

The next year he is granted a teaching assistantship. It's an awkward job, given his mixed successes at writing. He follows the text and borrows classroom strategies from more experienced TAs. There is success. He is well liked. But he knows that he doesn't know what he is doing.

The local Thriftway. Pays for groceries with food stamps. The checker is a former student who throws him a set of keys: "Take a look at my new BMW." Victor steals the grocery cart to get food and diapers home. There is envy, a sense that something isn't right, but he knows he'd rather teach than check groceries.

In his class, a Mexican American student, dressed in an ROTC uniform, writes about his grandmother's gibberish. "Gibberish" is the word he uses to define a language the student doesn't understand. The student writes another paper about the deterrent necessity of nuclear stockpiling. Another student, after reading *Catch-22,* explains how Yossarian is simply a coward. There's something "off" about the student's writing, apart from his sensibility. The sensibility troubles Victor, but not inordinately: Victor knows about the headlong drive to assimilate. That isn't the wrong that he can't pin down. Victor can't pin down what's off about the writing itself.

Another Mexican American, in another class, approaches Victor after class, carrying his copy of *Fahrenheit 451,* required reading for the course. The student doesn't understand the reference to a *salon.* Victor explains that this is just another word for the living room. No understanding in the student's eyes. He tries Spanish: *la sala.* Still nothing. The student had grown up as a migrant worker. And Victor remembers the white student who had been in his class a quarter ago, who had written about not understanding racism, that there was none where he had grown up, in Wennatchee, that he had played with the children of his father's migrant workers without there being any hostility. His father's workers. Property. Property that doesn't know of living rooms. And Victor thought of what the man from Wennatchee knew, what the ROTC Mexican American knew, what the migrant worker knew. And he thought of getting up the next morning to go with Serena to St. Mary's for cheese and butter. And he knew there was something he was not doing in his composition classrooms.

VI Of Color, Classes, and Classrooms

Hot, bright, stage lights blaring down on the four teachers and two parents seated in a circle before a TV camera. The six are about to speak on the cable network's public access channel.

Channing is the ring leader. He is a big man, large, round face with a shock of rumpled gray hair, a large belly pressing on a gray vest, not the rotund of the sedentary, but the large of the powerlifter. He is big, blustery, and brilliant: a polymath, well-versed in everything it seems, another who had traveled the class system: a childhood of unusual affluence, son of a government ambassador, an adulthood of unusual poverty.

There is Jolinda. She is lovely, thin, with shoulder-length auburn hair, sparse make-up. She has a quick, critical mind—decisive, unflinching. A long-time interracial marriage and a racially mixed child to raise keeps her decidedly active politically, a hard-working Democrat for Jesse Jackson's Rainbow Coalition, a hard-working advocate for her children's school.

David Zank, goatee, beret, an administrator and a teacher at Jolinda's and Channing's and Victor's children's school. He administers an alternative public school. It's an elementary school, one not divided into traditional grades, though the students tend to group themselves into the younger, the older, the middle kids. It's a school that attracts children from all of the city's classes and races. Instead of a set curriculum, children decide on projects of interest, the teachers providing all that is necessary to carry out the projects: the mechanics, say, of building an airplane, lessons on aerodynamics, on the history of experiments in flight, and so on, though this ideal isn't always reached. Discipline is handled through "forum": students, teachers, and parents in a circle to discuss injustices. Injustices, not rules—there are no rules, really, but infringements on what is generally held to be socially acceptable behavior. Anyone can call for a forum. Issues are discussed. The school is democracy in action, not the usual contradiction of an authoritarian structure preaching democracy. Zank is an instrumental part of that school.

There are also two teachers from one of the more traditional public schools in the area. Their names are now forgotten, our being together limited to that one show. Channing had found them. Silver gray hair on both, off the neck, tastefully curled atop heads, the look of professional coiffeurs. They have stylish glasses, pleasant faces. Both are part of this discussion before the camera because they are upset by recent changes in their curriculum, changes imposed from above, from higher administration.

And there is Victor, graduate student, parent.

Channing opens the discussion. At issue is a new curriculum the city has purchased from a major publishing house. It's a computerized package. Depending on how they perform on a standardized pretest, students are presented with a series of hierarchically ordered mastery tests. Versions of a mastery test are taken and retaken until a certain score is attained; then students are directed to the next test, which is taken, retaken again, until a certain score is reached; then onto the next, and so on. The guarantee of the package is that there will be a city-wide improvement on national standardized scores, a guarantee that will be made good, no doubt. But the teachers protest that all curricular decisions are thereby taken from them, that they will be able to do nothing but teach to tests.

Zank's school has annually refused to administer standardized tests on the grounds that even though they measure nothing but the ability to take tests they are too easily read as matters of intellectual ability by the students themselves. He tells the teachers to do the same as his school's teachers—refuse to take part. The teachers say that though they agree with Zank on principle, they cannot afford to jeopardize their jobs. They would not have the support of their principal, would not enjoy the support of Zank's teachers. Jolinda argues that their jobs are the education of children—matters of public responsibility more than personal security. Again, there is agreement on principle, but personal security is not confined to any one individual; there are families to care for. Victor suggests not teaching *to* the tests, but teaching test-taking. His life would have been easier, perhaps, if he had understood standardized test-taking and knew not to take what they actually measure (test-taking) seriously. Zank nods, saying "Paulo Freire kind of stuff."

Victor had never heard of Paulo Freire before Zank's comment. He reads *Pedagogy of the Oppressed*. The things written there make sense. He sees what has been working in his children's school: children believing in their humanity, willing and able to take social responsibility, even at the age of six. He sees the problem he has had with the school, despite being pleased in the main: "laissez-faire." Here's Freire:

> I cannot leave the students by themselves because I am trying to be a liberating educator. Laissez-faire! I cannot fall into laissez-faire. On the other hand, I cannot be authoritarian. I have to be radically democratic and responsible and directive. *Not* directive of the *students,* but directive of the *process,* the liberating teacher is not doing something *to* the students but *with* the students. (Shor and Freire 46)

Students cannot be left to their own devices totally, yet they cannot be handed everything.

Fall 1984. Victor is placed in charge of the English department's basic-writing program. He is the best candidate for the job in a number of ways: his fields are rhetoric and composition; he is doing research that focuses on basic writing; he is of color in a program replete with students of color; and he is willing, as were the directors of the program before him, to undertake the job at teaching-assistant pay. Administration denies the color aspect. Tokenism, stereotyping—sensitive issues.

He institutes a Freire-like dimension to the curriculum. He does away with the focus on sentence-combining, adopts the autobiography of Carolina Maria deJesus, *Child of the Dark,* the story of a woman from the *favelas* of Brazil, where Freire had spent his adolescence, the likely nurturing ground for his pedagogy. Her diary presents a view from the eyes of a barely literate woman, her political awareness and the contradictions she embodies, her understanding of social stratification, and her desire for what she believes she cannot have, the social stigma she suffers in having to provide for her children by collecting trash, and the pride she nevertheless feels, the way she is labeled a Marxist by a local politician when she complains about her living conditions in a system she somehow believes in. It's the story of an American of color and of poverty set in Brazil. It is a story that the basic-writing students might well understand. And, because she is barely literate, the writing is such that the students can be critical of her language use, can gain confidence in their own abilities with literacy.

The basic-writing teachers seem to enjoy teaching the book. But the political is downplayed. Discussions turn on the cultural: "Tell me 'bout the ghetto and I'll tell you 'bout the 'burbs." Students enjoy the dialogue. But there seems to be no dialectic, no sustained probing into the conditions that relegate certain peoples to the ghettos and others to the 'burbs in disproportionate numbers. In some sense, this is a minor problem, outweighed by the students' being heard at all.

Still there are problems, not with the material but with the relations between students and teachers, the kinds of problems discussed by Lisa Delpit. Students are being graded on their courage more than on how others at a university or elsewhere might regard their writing. Disgruntled students complain that they have been lied to, that they thought they really were "A" or "B" writers, only to find that others consider them barely literate. Irate professors say that the university is no place for remedial courses. Victor convinces the higher administration that the basic-writing program is a cultural education, not remediation. The program survives, eventually acquiring a regular, permanent administrator.

But while Victor was still there, there were still the disgruntled and the irate to contend with. He prepares a memo that quotes Louis Faraq'an, a naive move. The memo notes that Faraq'an defines black power as the ability for black people to come to the table with their own food. The point is to have teachers stop proffering academic charity, no matter how well intentioned. Victor knew the pain of charity.

He goes on a job interview. He returns to find a memo announcing his replacement for the coming academic year. He had not been consulted. The rationale was that he would surely get a job. But he remembered the teachers' argument in that television show. He had gone too far.

There must be a way to go about doing our jobs in some traditional sense and meeting some of the potential inherent in our jobs, the potential for social change, without inordinately risking those jobs. Utopianism within pragmatism; tradition and change.

When I think of tradition, I think of the literary critic turned compositionist, turned social critic—E. D. Hirsch. His *Cultural Literacy* is simplistic and politically dangerous, say his critics in English studies (e.g., Bizzell, Johnson, and Scholes). There is surely the sense that he's suggesting a return to halcyon days that never were, surely not wondrous bygone days for people of color, surely not for the poor. Hirsch is among those who believe that "multilingualism is contrary to our traditions and extremely unrealistic" (93). More myth than history. It is this mythic nostalgia that permeates his book, that causes him to be read as advocating teaching a literary canon. He denies it (xiv). He says that he is advocating a national-cultural set of common assumptions to be learned through an understanding of national-cultural allusions, his list of "what literate Americans know," a list, he points out, containing relatively few references to literary works (146–215; xiv). But he apparently senses the superficiality, backing up his theory with references to broad reading (109, 23). What, then, to read? Seems like we're back to a canon.

And that canon has historically favored one gender and one race. That this is the case, says Hirsch, is an accident of history (106). He seems not to regard how that particular accident has had a high casualty count over time. And it keeps recurring—like the same fender-bender with the same car at the same intersection—time and again. But Hirsch does go on to argue that national-cultural allusions are subject to change, that as more women and people of color become literate, they will affect the norms. And there is something to this. There are more women in the canon nowadays, more people of color. But the changes are not proportionate to the accomplishments or the potentials of women or people of color, surely. And those who enter the canon tend to be those who are politically safe. We read Langston Hughes's "Theme for English B" more often than Hughes's more angry "The Negro Speaks of Rivers." We read Martin Luther King, Jr. but little of W. E. B. DuBois, Richard Rodriguez instead of Ernesto Galarza, Emily Dickinson more often than Virginia Woolf (see Aiken; West "Canon Formation"). Hirsch's hopes are for better test scores and for greater access to the middle class, not for making the class system more equitable.

For all that, there *is* something to cultural literacy. One has to know how to be heard if one is to be heard. Those who rail the loudest against cultural literacy can afford to. They already have it. How, then, to exploit it without being subsumed by it?

Critical literacy, like that espoused by Paulo Freire and others, will lead to change, we're told. And I agree with that too. But what are the students to be critical of? How do they come to know what to be critical of? Why not cultural literacy, the national culture? Play out the polemic; develop the dialectic.

One theorist who has seen the necessity for both the cultural and the critical is Antonio Gramsci. His theories will provide the focus of the next chapter. For now, it's enough just to mention that he was an advocate of teaching a national culture, of teaching the classics, of something that sounds a lot like cultural literacy. Yet Gramsci also added that the classics and the national-cultural should be taught in such a way as to expose what he called the folkloristic, the commonly accepted ways of the world, the things too often accepted as if they are a part of nature—in short, the ideological. This suggests to me that it is possible to provide what's needed for the commonly accepted notions of success but with a critical dimension that might foster social action among teachers and among students. This is what sociologist Stanley Aronowitz and educational theorist Henry Giroux call "the language of possibility" (138–62). This is likely what Freire alludes to when he writes of a pedagogy that pits permanence with change (*Pedagogy* 72). I prefer "tradition" to "permanence," given Hirsch's observation that traditions can and do change. Tradition and change for changes in traditions.

In a way, the graduate course on classical rhetoric I teach lends itself best to Gramsci's ideas. We read Plato, Aristotle, Cicero, Quintilian, and others. And we discuss and write about the ways in which some of the things they espoused are still with us—things like censorship for children's better good; things like the only meaningful language should be on abstractions rather than concretes. Plato and the rhetoric of the constitution. We find the first-century idea of proper oratorical arrangement and discover the basis for the five-paragraph theme. We find Cicero writing of writing as a mode of learning and Quintilian writing of peer-group work. We look at how the ancients are still with us and question the degree to which they ought to be. Students gather something of a classical education, a matter of some prestige, and they develop a critical perspective.

Something of the same ideas can be adapted for undergraduates, secondary students, elementary students.

1990, Flagstaff: Victor and Carol's younger children attend the public school. The school district has adopted a literacy package from a major publishing house that explicitly discourages individual instruction. All the children perform their drills in unison, do their reading together—everybody, every time, getting 100 percent on everything. This isn't a matter of collaboration. Just recitation. No talking to neighbors seated ten inches away; no looking at neighbors. The books contain color: drawings of kids with nappy hair or slant eyes, not caricatures, done respectfully; yet there is a single cultural norm being advanced—force-fed cultural literacy.

More than hints at racism start to crop up at home. The brown-skinned, curly haired five-year-old daughter asks whether an Indian woman (the largest number of people who are of color in the community) would care for a human baby if she found one. A human baby! Another daughter, seven at the time, considerably more immersed in this literacy package than the kindergartner, mentions in passing that she doesn't care for black people. She doesn't know any. And she fails to see her own sister's features, forgets the pictures of her aunt, on whom the West African comes out clearly.

Victor and Carol don't blame the school completely. Market forces have them living in a predominately white community, making for little exposure to the kind of cultural complexity Victor and Carol's older children had known in Seattle or that Victor had known as a child in New York. But even if the school was not completely to blame for the hints at racism Victor and Carol would now have to counter, there remained the school's blind acceptance of a reductive notion of cultural literacy, a presentation that did nothing to expose and glory in difference as well as similarity.

Home schooling becomes the only short-term (and economically viable) alternative. Victor and Carol expose the national-cultural, but with an eye to multiplicity. The seven-year-old reads Cinderella, for instance. But she doesn't just stop with the Disney version. She reads translations of the Grimm Brothers' version, Poirot's seventeenth-century French version, an older Italian version, an ancient Chinese version. They're readily available. Discussion concerns how different people, with different ways and living in different times, can see some of the same things differently. She writes her own Cinderella story, which inevitably includes characters and situations from her own life. Spelling comes from the words she's trying to use in her own writing. It has a context. Grammar comes from trying to make her stories sound like she wants them to.

Other subjects take a similar tact. For history and geography, for example, she reads stories of dragons from China and dragons of the middle ages and dragons of C. S. Lewis and even dragons of Homer. She writes dragon stories.

Oral proficiency more or less takes care of itself; no need to impose doggedly the standard dialect. Victor's dialect changed without his being overtly conscious of it. The Spanish accent that Sister Rhea Marie had long ago warned his parents about disappeared, as did much of the black dialect he had acquired on the block. The more he became exposed to written discourse, the more his speaking came to reflect that exposure. And exposure to different worldviews, even if written in one standard dialect, provided the critical perspective. Reading aloud would help hone speaking skills in the prestige dialect.

I take the Cinderella idea to high school and college. The only real difference in the high school and the college is that I have the college students look up and report on literary critics who write about fairy tales. They read people like Bruno Bettelheim, who comes up with crazy interpretations of Cinderella as going through Freudian puberty rites, or others who write about fairy tales and archetypes, or Plato and his notion that fairy tales should be used to indoctrinate children into proper attitudes about life and the gods. I have the students do research about the historical or cultural conditions which existed at the time and place of the various versions. They become exposed to academics and academic discourse using a kind of literature they know intimately. They feel comfortable being critical of the great authorities. With the junior high and high school kids I've visited on short stints, I have provided the histories and selected the critical analyses; otherwise, the assignments have been the same.

Students resist being critical of fairy tales. They want to say that fairy tales are simply diversions for children. And this is okay as a jumping-off point for discussion. Resistance is a good thing, an assertion of authority, an opening for dialogue (see Giroux). So it tends that through the dialogue some begin to question what else might be contained in those simple diversions. A student writes about Rosie the Riveter during World War Two, women not just entering male-domi-nated jobs, like business and medicine, but performing "man's work," physical labor—and doing well. Then she wonders at Disney's Cin-derella, which promotes the house wench whose only hope for the future is to marry well. She wonders if Disney's version didn't help put Rosie's daughters "back in their place." Another writes about the Chinese version, about foot binding as a way to keep women in their place. She wonders if having Cinderella wear glass is a kind of modern foot binding. Another notices how Red Riding Hood's stories become more and more sexual as they approach the Victorian era. Another student: Is Jack and the Beanstalk a promotion of laissez-faire eco-nomics, get rich however you can? Is Robin Hood a proto-socialist? Students look at fairy tales and children's stories, and, in looking, begin to question the obvious and the natural, begin to question ideology.

Another way we look at ideology is by using Roland Barthes's little book *Mythologies*. The book contains a series of articles Barthes had written for a popular French magazine in the 1950s. Here, again, the idea works for high school and for college. The college students are asked to read and work with the theoretical essay at the end of the book, where Barthes explains semiology. Others get the idea without the thick theoretical language. But I want to introduce the college students to the esoteric language of "pure" theory. They resist—vehemently. There was outright mutiny in one class.

But, generally, they do tend to respond well to the essays. In one essay, for example, Barthes explains the popularity of professional wrestling as a spectacle, as containing the elements of ancient Greek plays. Students get the notion of the spectacle. One student writes about how wrestling in the 1990s exploits stereotypes, exploits and promotes existing prejudices. A videotape of contemporary wrestling backs him up. In terms of ideological mythologies, another student, a retired policeman, writes about TV ads to help the hungry as maintaining the myth of American prosperity. The poor and hungry children are in Latin America or in Africa, never dying of hunger and disease in America's cardboard shacks. A sophisticated literary theory is introduced—traditional academic discourse—and critical questioning arises— a possibility for change.

The basic idea is to present the cultural in such a way as to have students question worldviews, become critical. Action presupposes a need for action. Questioning what is commonly accepted makes clear the need for action. Among the things that are commonly accepted is the canon.

Literature can be set up so as to create a dialectic between differing worldviews, between the national-cultural and the critical. Students read Hemingway, for example, as male, white, middle-class as they come, skeptical, perhaps, but no radical. Then they read Buchi Emecheta's *Double Yoke*—the story of a black African woman trying to get through different value systems, cultures, different ways of viewing the world, her struggles at gaining a college degree. Men and women are at issue, black and white; the tribal ways that the main character, Nko, was raised with against the modern Western ways of the university. White students confronting the college community, women, African American students, American Indian students—all have a portion of Nko's pains, and, since the story takes place far away, the defense of bigotries does not come up immediately, as it often does in more explicitly African American or Latino or American Indian literature (though it is good to have these prejudices present themselves). Nko and Hemingway's Nick Adams handle things differently, confront different obstacles. Ideologies peep out of the classroom discussions (which usually begin with moral questions: Nick's sense of responsibility, Nko's integrity). What is it about where the characters come from that causes them to behave and believe in different ways? We can look at Steinbeck and Ayn Rand, Rodriguez and Galarza, Louis L'Amour and Leslie Marmon Silko. Students sometimes shock themselves with their own prejudices—anti-color *and* anti-white.

The students write about how they too must confront conflicts, and about the sources of those conflicts. These aren't always explained in grand cultural terms, but the cultural is always present, often coming out in discussions. They write autobiographies (or narratives if culturally uncomfortable with the autobiographic). The things they are to write about concern their own experiences, experiences that are tied to the things they are reading. Toward the end of the semester they are asked to downplay the autobiographical elements but keep them in mind. The autobiographical is an important assessment tool, even essential— always there, really. "[A]ll writing, in many different ways, is autobiographical," says Donald Murray, even "academic writing, writing to instruct, textbook writing" (67; 73). But outside the English classroom the autobiographical, the narrative, is not usually appreciated (Spellmeyer). So we look at how the personal is impersonally imparted in writing, still looking to different worldviews espoused in standard written form. We look at Booker T. Washington and W. E. B. DuBois, then find out about their backgrounds, how two African Americans living in the same time can come to polar viewpoints. Or we look at Martin Luther King, Jr. and Malcolm X. In a sense, the strategy is not much different from that proposed by David Bartholomae and Anthony Petrosky: an investing of the personal into what is read and an investigation into how what is read appears, its presentation. The difference is in the introduction of difference within convention. Throughout, there are the culturally literate and the critical, both in what they read and in what they write.

Some students—even a lot, even those who come from poor minority backgrounds—reject the critical views. This is to be expected. People are not turned around overnight. Floyd, back in Kansas City, showed that. But the goal is not necessarily to have students relinquish national-cultural myths. The goal is to expose them to differences and similarities within the literacy conventions they have to contend with, to know the traditional norms while also appraising them, looking at the norms critically. It's a directed process, not propaganda.

All of this is to say that it is possible to have our educational cake and eat it too. It is possible to do our jobs as others define them: provide *haute couture,* "high literacy," literacy skills, standardized-test-ready cultural literacy. And it is possible to do our jobs as we believe they ought to be done: with students recognizing that education should carry social responsibility. We can do critical literacy. And what better to be critical of than the cultural norms contained in tradition? Start with what students know or have been told they ought to know. Allow and encourage a questioning of the norms. And maybe look to how things might be—and ought to be—changed.

The need for social action was clear enough to see for the graduate student reading what professionals in composition were saying about basic writers, most often students of color. Clearly intelligent people, clearly compassionate people, some of whom he has come to know and to like, were writing some politically questionable things.

His first intensive reading of academics on composing centered on speaking and writing, orality and literacy, and questions of cognitive competence. Although the researchers and the theorists he read then have moved on to other issues or have altered their positions as the profession has moved away from a focus on cognition to a focus on the social, there are still teachers he comes into contact with who have not moved on. And some of the concerns which arose with the cognitive have not been removed by the shift to the social: the focus on difference defined in exclusively racial and cultural terms. There is also class.

So he enters his first research project. He wants to begin by breaking away from the suggestion that students of color are basic writers exclusively. Some do go on. Some students of color are never assigned to basic-writing courses. And he wants to break away from the oral-literate, speaking-writing dichotomy. His initial research question asks how basic writers of color differ from traditional writers of color, and whites, in terms of reliance on oral language features in writing. He looks to writing groups, where speaking, listening, writing, and reading interact.

The research.

Talk within groups is recorded using lapel microphones and a sound mixer. The focus is on students' readings of their own texts and the discussions which follow. The recordings are then transcribed and coded. The coding is an adaptation of procedures developed by Wallace Chafe and by Deborah Tannen. Both are sociolinguists who see speaking and writing as different in both strategies and conventions. The transcriptions and the students' written texts are analyzed with respect to breakdowns in the flows of speech: the flubs and false starts, the "ums," "ahs," and stammers of speech—"mazes" (Fagan). Mazes would betray disjunctures between what is written and what is read, where the oral-aural and the written don't jibe.

There are four groups: two basic, two traditional. There are twelve students: five in the basic writing course, seven in the more traditional freshman composition course. The twelve represent a racial and cultural mix. Among the basic are an American Indian from Alaska; a Latina of Filipina, Spaniard, and Irish descent; a white woman, according to surname, raised by her Mexican-American mother; a woman from Southeast Asia; a Saipanese man. There are no African American students enrolled in the basic writing class. The traditional students include only three who are literally traditional: white, male, and middle class. The rest include an African American woman, a Japanese American woman from Hawaii, a white man raised by his Filipina mother, and a Jewish woman who was raised alongside her adopted African American sister. Apart from what would be expected of the two immigrant students in the basic-writing course, no student speaks in a noticeably nonstandard dialect. Personal backgrounds and discourse histories are gathered through interviews. Everything is tabulated. Basic writers are significantly less oral than the traditional students. Differences are tabulated; charts and tables produced.

But let's bypass "data" here and look at some illustrative students instead. Some of the marks which act as inflectional markers are

/   the short pause of a written comma

//   the longer pause of written period

:   stretching out the final sound ("heyy")

::   really stretching out the final sound ("heyyy")

These symbols show up when comparing what is read with what is written. When transcribing conversation, conventional punctuation is used, though signifying inflections more than written-discourse conventions. All this will become clear very quickly in what follows.

Lori was a student in the traditional freshman composition course. At the time of the research, 1985, she was a nineteen-year-old sophomore, Japanese American, born and raised in Hawaii. Her parents are native to Hawaii, her great-grandparents from Japan. Lori heard some Japanese spoken at home, but as far as she is concerned she is monolingual in English.

Both her parents work outside the home. Lori sees her mother and father as middle class. Her mother "does a lot of computer things." As for her father:

> My dad is a machinist for boats, down at Hawaii Fishing Boats that bring in tuna. They have a tuna factory down the way, and he fixes all the boats. I think he was a rookie at about age fifteen. But now he's kinda like a supervisor there. S'been there forty years. He's like. They don't know him by his real name. Junior's what they call him.

"They don't know him by his real name"—after forty years at the same workplace. Lori, like others among the traditional course, associates class with earnings. She ranks her father as white collar, not skilled labor. He and his wife had raised Lori in a single-family dwelling, had managed to assure her attendance at an exclusive private school from kindergarten through the twelfth grade. Lori sees herself as from the middle class.

And in seeing herself as middle class her perceptions of class and color become blurred. When describing her school, for example, she begins by identifying the school as predominantly white, but the more she speaks, the more the identification became questionable:

> It's mainly a Caucasian school. But when I was there. I mean there's enough Asian students that I don't. I never thought about it. Another private school is considered an Oriental, an Asian school. But when you go there, the people who visit the school, they are surprised how many white students there are. It's just that type of image. But when you go there, there's equal amount. I guess that's how it was where I go, went, too.

She had attended a predominantly white school that might have been equally Asian.

School included a good deal of English courses: vocabulary lists, grammar drills, a year of creative writing, no composition courses. Reading consisted of "the kind of stuff you need for college." Though Lori was not read to at home, she was required to undertake home reading—aloud:

> When I was small, my father used to make me read out loud to get me to read. Oh yes. He used to correct my intonations, like with question mark, colon, period. I was supposed to take a breath afterward. It was those kind of things. It was like those *See Spot Run* books.

Even at home, literacy was skills-oriented and conventional: traditional reading, innocuous readers. She was well-prepared for correct college writing. As she would hear papers read aloud in the group, she would comment with "There's one sentence that sounded like a run-on" or with "the paragraph in there . . . ," even though there was no text before her. She could "see" the punctuation in what she heard.

Most of her mazes reflected the detection of errors rather than substantive reconsiderations of text:

> *Draft:* The new occupants are an old fashion couple where the husband is the man of the house and wife is suppose to belong in the kitchen.
>
> *Spoken:* My new occupants are::/an old-fashioned couple/where the husband is the man?
>
> ((to the group)) I guess the husband would be the man of the house. Maybe quotes, so that she ((the instructor)) can see that *I* see the logic. Anyway::/My new occupants are an old-fashioned

couple where the husband is the man of the house and the wife//
the wife is supposed to belong in the kitchen.

Minor matters. But they hint at her culture and of her being a traditional
writer. The missing inflectional ending in "old-fashion" or "suppose
to" and the missing article before "wife" are like the kinds of errors
one would expect of an Asian learning English as a foreign language
(Liem). Yet the tell-tale signs of a first language other than English
only occur in her writing. Aloud, she pronounces the *-ed*; aloud she
betrays some surprise at having missed the article before "wife." As far
as Lori is concerned, the errors are no more than that, slips, not a
reaching back to some archaic memory of a first language now forgotten:

> *Me:* In this draft here, it struck me that some of the errors, some
> of the stuff you revised out, were like the kinds of things you'd
> expect from Asian students coming to English for the first
> time. Did you notice them in that way? I mean like an accent?
>
> *Lori:* No. They're just. I'm just kind of. I just don't worry when
> I'm writing a rough draft.... I just write real fast, and you
> know you can clean it up later.

For Lori, the errors are the result of quick first-draft writing. Lori, like
the other traditional writers, allows oral features to appear in first drafts;
in her case, the oral including some dialect traces. Lori, like the
traditional typically, moves from the oral-like to the more literate.

Also in a manner typical of the traditional, Lori's moves to the
literate are motivated to great extent by a desire to meet teacher
expectations. She even says, "Maybe I better think of the teacher as
the audience." At one point in particular, Lori makes clear how much
she and her group consider the teacher, despite an understanding of
oral-literate differences that is sufficiently sophisticated to affect the
teacher.

Lori is commenting on a draft of a paper written by another member
of the Group, Willy. The draft had already been commented on by
Elizabeth, the instructor, a graduate student of medieval literature.
Elizabeth's comments on Willy's paper concern passive constructions
and clichés. Lori says to the group,

> Yeah. Like, our assignment was to write a letter to. You're, telling,
> you know, pretty closely. And everyone you write, to a friend,
> you use different language. You talk on paper, like. And you're
> saying that now because it's a paper assignment you go over it
> in stages of rewrite. We're going over it to catch *clichés* and *to-
> be verbs*. And we're saying. Well, *I'm* saying if you are writing to
> a friend, it's different than when you're writing considerations of
> the person, I mean like the teacher. So, okay, how's she going to

grade things. How's she going to handle clichés, or maybe things
she doesn't understand because that person is a very close friend.

Lori and others in the overall discussion explicitly point to the ways
in which a personal letter is more oral-like than literate, how clichés
are instances of interpersonal involvement, oral, with Wallace Chafe
classifying the interpersonal devices, like the cliché, as an oral-language
feature. And she discusses the artificiality of the teacher's assignment
and how to adjust accordingly. The traditional composition students
are very conscious of oral and literate differences, can play with those
differences, though always within rules established by the teacher.

Edita was a member of the basic-writing class. She is a twenty-nine-
year-old freshman. Her ethnic background is Filipino and Latino on
her father's side, Irish-English on her mother's. Edita's mother had
raised her since she was twelve. Edita nevertheless considers herself
Latina. Her mother had never worked outside the home, taking in
laundry, ironing, sewing, other odd jobs, turning to state aid when
necessary. Edita's high school had a 51.4 percent minority enrollment
in 1983 (Superintendent 24), a majority of minorities. She had graduated
a few years before she entered college.

Memories of school-directed writing or reading are few. She remembers having written some stories in grade school and having written
one book report during junior high. She could recall no required writing
in high school. Edita had not done much reading on her own either.
Nor had she heard reading aloud in her childhood. At home, rules
were to be followed without objection or comment. She said her
upbringing made her "a real introvert." Yet apart from a stretch of
giggling during the first recorded writing-group session, she didn't seem
at all introverted.

Edita's mazes and subsequent changes to her texts reveal an inap-
propriate attention to literate strategies. Syntactically, she produces
mazes in noting simple editorial matters:

> *Draft:* I learned the hard way the importance of school in higher
> education.
>
> *Spoken:* I learned the hard way the importance of school i:/uh::/
> and/higher education.
>
> *Revised:* I learned the hard way the importance of school and
> higher education.

Or she reconsiders punctuation:

> *Draft:* We thought it was great, however, while. . . .

Spoken: We thought/it was *great*//mm:/bu/however what

Revised: We thought it was great. However, what. . . .

Edita changes the punctuation to fit her delivery, trusting her ear in a relatively small matter. More transpires, however. Along the way she betrays an impulse to use "but." But there is an informality to *but.* *But* is often a simple phatic utterance in speaking, a filler, a sound to help keep the discourse moving. Edita, it appears, thinks *but* too informal, too much like talk. She does not surrender to the oral impulse betrayed by the maze.

A tendency to reject the oral-like shows in broader syntactic concerns. In one instance, she finds herself opening sentences with the same phrase. Edita's response is to attempt more complex subordinating sentences, greater integration, a literate feature according to Chafe:

> *Draft:* I am taken away by the tranquil atmosphere. I am taken away by the extra-ordinary, natural beauty of it's desert-like atmosphere.
>
> *Spoken:* I am taken away by the tranquil//um//tranquil/um:/ atmosphere?//((silence: 12 secs.))I am:/I am taken away by the extraordinary natural beauty of its desert-like atmosphere//
>
> *Revised:* When I come here, the thoughts and pressure that I have in the city soon leave me as I am taken away by the tranquil atmosphere and extraordinary beauty.

Neither draft seems particularly oral-like. The repetition could make for an effective stylistic device. Yet the elaboration and subordination is more literate-sounding. The more literate-like the better, evidently.

In another instance, however, Edita runs into problems:

> *Draft:* Somehow, we slipped though the cracks the school system set up for us.
>
> *Spoken:* Somehow we slipped through the cracks::/the school system set up to help us//
> ((To the group)) No. That isn't it. I mean, they didn't set *up* the cracks; we slipped *through* them. I don't know.
>
> *Revised:* Somehow, we slipped through the cracks that the school system had set up to help us.

Edita senses the metaphorical and logical problems. In an attempt to rectify, she changes "for us" to "to help us." When that doesn't seem to do the job she tries adding "that." But she never tries talking out the sentence. She is text-bound. Syntactically, Edita tends not to trust her oral impulses.

Rhetorically, Edita's revisions concern finding proper levels of elaboration. Edita begins with what she would decide is too much information, then cuts back, a constant reassessment of audience:

> *Draft:* I had a special group of friends composed of four people plus myself, who, had the same problem I had about school.

> *Spoken:* I had a group of friends composed of four://of four people plus my self/who had the same problem I/I did// ((To the group)) I guess John ((the instructor)) will get it, huh. I mean about school, and like that. I mean, he. Never mind.

> *Revised:* I had a group of four friends plus myself, who had the same problems I did.

The rhetorical issue is tied to Edita's sense of a distance between her experiences and those of her instructor.

More than once, her comments on others' papers, or in defense of her own to the group, center on what the instructor would likely know. Edita comments on a paper by SreyNun, who had written of her experiences in coming to America from Cambodia without her parents:

> *Edita:* So your parents weren't in that camp with you?

> *SreyNun:* No. No. I have three sister and two brothers that

> *Edita:* You have to make that clear, that you had no choice. It's that. Oh::. I don't want to sound like a jerk. But sometimes people, here, send their kids away on vacations and like that. Summer camps to Mexico. Like that. I don't know. I think you should make it clearer. . . . I mean I like John and all, but he isn't going to know a lot about how::/about being with noth:. I'm talking too much.

John is their comp teacher, sitting at the front of the class, or else roaming about, a Groucho Marx-like fellow, a Groucho fan at that, immediately likeable. He is a graduate student of poetry, an experienced secondary-school teacher who had even spent some time as a school principal. Edita never finishes her comment on what John would not know. Yet she does specify John, not the group. No other member of the group would know of a young refugee's experiences. But all of the members would know "about being with noth[ing]." Add the reference to those who can afford to send their children on far-off vacations, and it becomes clear that Edita is thinking along economic lines.

One more illustration. The essay under discussion is Edita's, an essay describing her experiences in school and within the job market. The other members are Diana, SreyNun, and Amo. Diana is a Mexican American woman, not interviewed, though it comes out in group conversations that she had lived in the same general area as Edita and had attended the same school as Edita, though a few years later. Amo is native Alaskan, a high school dropout, once nominated for public office, though he declined the nomination for fear that his limited literacy would be discovered.

Amo: That. I thought *that* was your best paper. That you told your life's story in a very short time.

Diana: That's hard.

Amo: And you went into stuff that college ki. Um. I don't know. Yeah. Showed, showed to me your dri::ve, your determination. You kind of expressed the way you feel about your school. You, you discovered a feeling you had inside that helped you in all your jobs. And it put you above all the rest of those, *people* around

Edita: Sure did.

Amo: You really describe for people who couldn't know the feelings, being sh::. Being pushed in the dummy section. Self-esteem. Being poor and being dumb. The paper gives me a ree/ an understanding.

Diana: I think you should, uh, I don't know. It sort of confuses me about your son. It's like you jus:: started your paper over. It's the feeling I get. It's the sound of it, I guess. I don't know how to say it.

Amo: Just say it.

Diana: I mean, it, it's good, but then at the end, you saying that the reason. You know? You want your son to do what you did. Right? The ending was confusing to me.

Edita: No, I don't.

Diana: I mean, like, you didn't just put it there, but I didn't quite get it. I mean, I mean, I understand what you are saying about your son but I don't know. I don't know if I.

Edita: Yeah, sometimes it's hard. I know what you mean. But, um, but, you see, when you got kids

Amo: It is that she. I can see the completeness, how it all fits into the, to your, what the message is to us. That just cause you're in college and computers and all, that the same thing could happen to your son, cause there still isn't the money so there's still the color or something. I, I *thought* that.

Diana: I mean like. You came out with a beginning. You should say something about your son then. I don't know if that would help.

Amo: Yeah, that could've been good. I, a good idea at the beginning. Your, you know, your theme.

> *Diana:* I mean cause it, it's, you just brought it, about your son. You're talking about yourself all the way through, and then you bring your son in, in addition.
>
> *Edita:* Yeah. But my *purpose* was *not* to talk about him at *all*. But my experience, the things *you* guys can fol, can understand, what you guys know something about, and how my experience would *change*, in, the way I would, raise *my* kid. So I have to talk about *my* self. Cause maybe in some way *we're* alike, but I'm not talking to *you*. I'm talking to people like *John* who don't move up from where we do. I wasn't talking about him. I was talking about myself. I think.

SreyNun, from a decidedly different social structure than the others, one which was in flux throughout her life, takes no part in the group's discussion. Diana might have had some things in common with Edita, but Diana is a recent high school graduate, considerably younger than Edita or Amo, only now living on her own. Diana's concerns are more conventionally student-like, text-centered, concerned with arrangement, the organization of Edita's essay.

Amo and Edita have class-related experiences in common. They both have living as adults in poverty in common. Culturally, they're quite different. Edita, the inner city, an Anglo-Latina mix; Amo, tribal life, with the Anglo influence more Canadian than American:

> *Diana:* Are you from Alaska?
>
> *Amo:* Yeah. But a lot of how we do things is on the Canadian side, kind of different from here or like Fairbanks.

Class, more than culture, binds Amo and Edita.

Edita simply trails off in her attempt to tell Diana about the perspective that comes with being an adult who has had working-class-related experiences and has a child. Amo understands Edita, how raising children is less at issue than explaining the difficulties in attempting to move within the class structure, the difference between "[b]eing poor and being dumb." Even Amo's reference to race is more a matter of class, a play on the cliché that money knows no color: "There still isn't the money so there's still the color." Amo ends the conversation on Edita's essay with a note of support, given a particular worldview:

> *Amo:* Well. Well. *Still*. You know, it's just the point of view. Because I. It fit in. The boy fit in. Uh. Your whole attitude about life now. You're treating him as basically your own attitude about college, about studying. It gave me a sense of completeness.

This is the view from the bottom of the class structure.

Writing and revising, for Edita, involves constant attempts at coming across as literate, to the point of neglecting or rejecting words or phrases that she might have considered conversational, oral-like. That this almost single-minded concern with the literate sometimes fails her betrays her relative lack of exposure to written discourse. That she is conscious of how systemic forces can shape experience is reflected in her discussion of larger rhetorical matters contained in the texts under group discussion, discussions concerned with what a middle-class audience would not know.

All of this takes me to the sociolinguist Basil Bernstein, to his theories on speech codes and social class, though with important differences when it comes to the American college classroom. In Bernstein's social matrix, a strictly hierarchical authority structure in the working-class' workplace gives rise to a hierarchical authority structure in the home. Authority is position-centered, more a matter of rank than of potential competence. Although there is no reason to presuppose that this reproduction is intentional, the nature of work involved in physical labor would affect home life, a sense that there isn't the time or that there aren't the conditions which allow for negotiation. Constraining conditions would be more pointed in a single-parent household. The majority of the basic writers in the research study came from single-parent households. All but one came from working-class households; all but one were not encouraged to speak out.

It would be safe to assume that those who find it necessary to work at physical labor would not feel at ease with their abilities at literacy practices. It would be understandable, then, that literacy concerns would be relegated to the schools. No reading was evident in all but one of the basic writers' homes, nor was reading aloud. For Amo, for example, reading aloud seemed almost a foreign concept:

Me: Has anyone ever read to you aloud regularly?

Amo: What?

Me: Aloud. Out loud.

Amo: Regularly? Depends on what you mean. Oh, yeah. Yeah. I mean, I remember in Alcoholics Anonymous we had to read this literature before we'd get started and so. Sometimes I read it. Usually every meeting we had to do that. It's from the main text. And they read it out loud. And everybody listens. Same book, same.

Me: How 'bout as a child?

Amo: What.

Me: Were you read to?

Amo: Out loud? Na. Sometimes my father would read something from the paper. But he didn't get the paper all that much. And he didn't read all that well. My mother never learned to, I don't think. I mean, what does a flicker need to read for? You know?

His mother never worked outside the home. His father was a laborer in a fish-processing plant. Amo's was a working-class, position-centered home.

Position-centered households make for a restricted speech code, according to Bernstein. As in oral-discourse strategies, shared social context among speakers is assumed within the restricted code. Because meaning is implicitly understood, discourse is fragmented. Meaning is particularistic, in Bernstein's terms. Much of this was seen in the interactions between Amo and Edita, in their understanding each other yet taking time to explain things to Diana. But Diana was not wholly "other." She was included in "the things . . . you guys know something about."

With Edita's and Amo's talk to Diana, however, comes a twist to Bernstein's theory. Members of the position-centered move away from the restricted code when they perceive themselves as no longer within their more familiar place within the class system. More elaboration became necessary for the instructor's sake. They assumed he was from the middle class.

Elaboration marks the speech code of the middle class, an elaborated code, in Bernstein's terms. The workplace and preparing children for survival in the workplace (even if not always a consciously child-rearing strategy) determines the code. In the middle-class workplace, authority boundaries are not drawn as clearly as they are in the physical-labor workplace. Some negotiation is possible: the committee replaces the suggestion box; explained tardiness replaces the punch clock. So authority in the household becomes person-centered. Some negotiation becomes possible; rules can sometimes be bent, given a well-formed, well-articulated argument. The elaborated code is explicit, context-free. It is universalistic, assuming little shared experience among speakers. The elaborated code parallels literate discourse.

Since the white-collar and the professional workplace depend upon literate practices, literacy instruction takes on special importance in the middle-class household. The middle class' speech code is the school's code.

Most of the students in the traditional course came from two-parent households, with both parents usually employed outside the house, performing white-collar or professional jobs. All of the traditional students could recall being encouraged to speak up at home. All had heard texts read aloud. All read at least magazines on their own. Lori believed she *heard* a run-on sentence, believed she heard a paragraph break.

In one exchange within Lori's group Hana comments on Willy's essay in decidedly literary terms:

> You need to do something about the first two sentences. They sound like Gothic novels. [laughter] Seriously. I get images of cliffs overlooking the sea. But it's only a stupid track meet. [laughter]

The group appreciates the comment. The writer understands it. Theirs is a literate background. Theirs is a consensus born of a common literate background.

This consensus again marks a twist on Bernstein's theories. For Bernstein, it should be the working class who bases social interaction on consensus. Social interaction among the middle class is supposed to be based on difference. If no context is assumed and must thereby be provided in an elaborated code, a commonality must not be assumed, Bernstein reasons. Yet the opposite took place in the college composition classrooms. The traditional students believed themselves to be of the same class as the majority within the academic community. The traditional—including the traditional of color—really did share in the speech code of the majority, a code having substantial similarities to literate written discourse. This sense of being essentially no different from others in the classroom's discourse community, which would include the teacher, made for a certain ease among the traditional students, an ease that was evident in their abilities at exploiting the oral-like in arriving at the literate.

The basic writers, on the other hand, were keenly aware of differences between themselves and the academic community. Nor was their focus on their cultural differences. In terms of culture, both classes were heterogeneous, albeit in different proportions (also connected to class, since fewer of color are to be found in the middle class generally). Class was the overriding difference between the basic writers and the community in which they found themselves. Their language might have been the same as the majority in the university's discourse community—English, even standard English, but the basic writers' class-structural determinants of speech code were different. This isn't dialect, remember. The basic writers spoke in the standard dialect. This is more like knowing how to talk, and about what, and how much.

The basic writers in this research study were at least implicitly aware of the discourse differences, denying their ways with oral discourse, attempting a somewhat foreign discourse pattern. The basic writers' problems were not rooted in an inordinate reliance on oral strategies; their problems came from their inordinate denial of the oral.

So where does all this lead? To the whole matter of classroom conversation and collaboration.

Collaboration in the traditional classroom tended to turn on matters of correctness, correctness seen in terms of the expectations of the academic community. For Kenneth Bruffee, the collaboration of writing groups allows group participants to enter into the conversation of a new community, with consensus as momentary stays in the conversation. The conversation and the consensus which result are, for Bruffee, parts of an actively democratic enterprise. All the students in a first-year college course are new members in a new community. So all are able to participate equally, the reasoning goes.

However, critics from the political left, like Greg Myers, fear that the consensus obtained in the classroom can be ideologically suspect. Consensus along the lines forwarded by Bruffee would not lend authority to voices of dissent or difference that the traditionally excluded in particular could provide. Consensus would threaten to push for agreement within current authority structures. New group members, white or of color, would be taking part in the ongoing conversation; they would not be joining to create or to change that conversation. In effect, critics fear, consensus would mean agreeing on what would satisfy long-time residents of the community—teachers. This is what happened among the traditional writers. Those with cultural differences quieted those differences. In effect, they became subject to acculturative and assimilationist forces. They became raceless.

John Trimbur argues that a way to avoid "spurious consensus," the agreement to conform, is to seek "utopian consensus." Utopian consensus does not assume that all members of the group or of the classroom community would necessarily come to agree on all matters (like what the teacher wants). Consensus would mean agreeing to recognize differences and similarities in worldviews, differences and similarities in individual and social experiences. In utopian consensus, the social and the political would be recognized. Individual*ism,* an ideological matter, could be countered. The individual (without the -ism), a human, subjective matter, would not be suppressed.

It was the basic writers who suggested utopian consensus in their group interactions. In the exchange concerning Edita's autobiographical essay, similarities among the members were acknowledged—and the differences: the things Diana would know and not know; the things the teacher would not know. Despite basic writers' problems with written discourse, there are lessons to be learned from them when it comes to group work.

The basic writers' group interactions suggest that composition studies' recent attention to acknowledging cultural difference in the composition classroom is as applicable to the traditional classroom as to the basic. Recognizing cultural differences would have students break from questionable class affiliations.

Only one among the traditional approached the cultural (read: "racism")—Hana, the woman who referred to Gothic novels in commenting on a peer's paper. Her autobiography focused on the different ways she and her adopted African American sister were treated outside the home, despite an identical cultural upbringing since infancy (to which the group reacted by pointing to word choice, mechanics, and the like). Hana alone pointed to the struggles different races face in our society. Yet there were others in that classroom likely to have had pointed experiences. Lori, for example, knew something of racism: her middle-aged, long-employed father, still called "Junior." All the students of color in the traditional writing course, without exception, shied away from the potentially confrontational, issues that might have questioned commonly held perceptions. The basic writers, on the other hand, were not disposed to denying difference—nor to denying that difference entails struggle. Their discussions underscore our need not only to acknowledge culture but to acknowledge class.

Class cannot be subsumed under culture without neutralizing the political dimension in education that can be acknowledged through writing groups. Confining discussions to matters of culture without considerations of class paints an ideological picture of a pluralism or a multiculturalism which does not yet exist in our society—and cannot exist without acknowledging the struggles inherent in the class system.

Linguistically, however, the basic writers in this study had taken difference to a point that threatened to work against them. In their latent recognition of the differences between their ways of speaking and their new community's ways, they made too much of oral-literate differences. Some of the basic writers' oral impulses could have improved their texts. With the possible exception of the two students who were relatively new to English, the basic writers did have a language in common with their instructor, speech-code differences notwithstanding. Sondra Perl long ago admonished teachers not to ignore "the highly elaborated, deeply embedded processes the [basic-writing] students bring with them. These unskilled writers," she went on, "are not beginners in the *tabula rasa* sense, and teachers err in assuming they are" (334). Basic-writing students themselves also commit such errors, evidently. The basic writers' problems might have been rooted in the differences between orality and literacy, but orality and literacy have the same root—language.

What the basic writers lacked was experience with the elaborated code, a code separated from literate written discourse by little more than minor conventions. George Dillon has claimed that one of the differences between better writers and the less able is that the better writers have an intuited sense of the sounds of written discourse: the traditional writers' abilities at discussing the sound of a sentence, a paragraph, a Gothic novel. We can introduce students to texts, read texts aloud, and nevertheless meet political aims and students' desires for an education that might provide the way for better lives. We can introduce the basic writers—and the traditional—to writers of color and from poverty who tell of their struggles, who tell of the politics, who attempt to counter the current hegemony, and who do so by exploiting oral and literate strategies in their writing in ways that meet the notions of competence which those who continue to dominate tend to require. We can make explicit that oral ways do have value, that professionals listen to the sound of their own discourse, even when that discourse is not intended to be read aloud (Cooper and Odell). Group work can focus writers on the sounds of their own discourse, calling attention to those falterings in their readings aloud of texts, calling attention to the suggestion that at some intuitive level writers might be considering a change, calling attention to their oral impulses. In short, basic writers can be encouraged to develop and to trust their oral and their literate ways while continuing to communicate the struggles entailed in being other-cultural and outside the middle class.

Victor struggles with the doctoral dissertation: not trusting in his Latino-literate, ostensibly oral ways, trying to maintain the voice of distance, of objectivity, of the researcher, without race, without a person. He believes he can.

And he believes he can teach, has come to believe he has something to teach as well: rhetoric as political, literacy as potentially powerful.

He goes on the round of job interviews, exhausting affairs, more than one person with which to interview. Misses one interview. Gets a call back. An interview-luncheon. Thick red wood and lush potted plants, rice pilaf and chicken breasts, exciting talk about rhetorical history and composition theories. In his mind's eye there is Carol in the one bedroom in south Seattle as he eats a posh meal and waxes intellectual. She has remained home with a twisted ankle, five dollars, four children, a door that won't lock properly, a utility shut-off notice in her hand. In the silence during bites, he thinks of the trip to the Salvation Army he will have to make upon his return, to beg for help with the utility shut-off, for a bag of food. He sells himself, his insecurities about the dissertation and anything else safely tucked away while talking. He had learned to be bad in scary situations long ago.

Victor lands a job. On to the middle class!

A friend lends the money with which to rent a car for the trip east. The car has to be large enough to belt in two adults and four children. It's a new Chrysler Fifth Avenue—finally, the bad ride, styling like the PR pimps who used to toss him a quarter for a buff shine. He knows he can't keep the car, but he wallows in the symbol of having made it.

Then the reality. Too much income to be on the state dole; not enough money to live much differently than before. The family moves into a rental in the Italian neighborhood that houses no Italians. He is among the white poor—more foreign than anything he had ever experienced. He knows fear in the streets for the first time, real fear, the fear whites must feel when they walk on *el bloque.*

Serena's friend, Jolinda's daughter, is coming to visit. Aviva has that beautiful coffee-with-cream brown of the *mulata,* curly hair, more nap than not. The house behind Victor and Carol's had had African American tenants for a very short time, weeks, gone during Christmas, days after their house had been broken into, "niggers" painted in red inside. Serena's one African American playmate in the Italian neighborhood was always escorted by her uncle, a huge man, shirtless, carrying a baseball bat. The couple next door had their pitbull dog, the dog that was smart because it hated niggers. Victor and family would have to move before Aviva's arrival.

They move into a middle-class area in a nearby city, Independence. More isolation. There is no neighborhood, just houses, garages opening mysteriously, sealed cars leaving, garages opening, cars returning. Pod people. At the public gathering places Victor is spoken to in Farsi one day, asked if he is from India the next. Victor the Curiosity. And he, himself, feels foreign. But the area is safe. None of the violence of the Italian neighborhood: the shooting Steven, the son, had witnessed; the police trying to shove a ten- or eleven-year-old-boy into one of the armored patrol wagons that cruised the neighborhood, and losing to the child, the boy who had simply gone to the police when beckoned, only to be grabbed, the boy stretching out his arms and legs to avoid getting thrown into the truck; the police helicopter's searchlight turning the night into day. No more. Just an eerie silence.

Safety has a price beyond isolation—literally a price. The phone is disconnected. The electricity is disconnected. For a time all cooking is on a barbecue. No gas. Water is heated in a stovetop oven, carried to the tub to provide hot baths for the babies. A spill; his legs scalded. Carol works on an assembly line making plastic dishes, works handing out free samples in a supermarket, on call, not enough to compensate for the cost of traveling to and from jobs, no tuition breaks for spouses with which to work toward a legitimate second income. Victor belongs to an economic class he hadn't known existed: the destitute-employed-professional.

His work has him festering in insecurity. There is grantsmanship. There is publication. There is still the dissertation. There is teaching graduate courses on writing when he still doesn't believe he knows how to write, when he is not yet legitimate, still fearing that he might not become legitimate, certified, the Ph.D.

The dissertation is complete. Revision decisions are handled over the phone: long trips from Independence to the office he shares with another, to use the office phone during the late night, his own phone having been disconnected, later to be charged for the calls. A trip back to Seattle to defend the dissertation, tense but not grueling, congratulations and handshakes, but not even the offer of a drink. Still the colored kid. A borrowed computer from folks in the Office of Minority Affairs, friends, to make last-minute changes required by the dissertation committee. To Channing's house, where friends from the neighborhood gather to congratulate and to celebrate. A call to Carol. She's in a flea-infested basement with the babies, shelter from a tornado whirling overhead. She and the babies should have been with him. But rent money had financed the trip. There would be the landlord to contend with upon his return from being granted the highest degree possible.

Now legitimate, he is offered a job he is not qualified for and is too insecure to decline—the Writing Project. The Saturdays he would have spent with his children are now spent traveling to teacher in-services, the teachers resenting their Saturdays gone as much as he, maybe more, given that they find him obscure, "too theoretical," a nice guy, but not in touch with the reality of the schoolroom. They are frustrated. They want gimmicks, things to do in the classrooms. He is frustrated. He believes a conceptual understanding provides the way for creating one's own gimmicks, gimmicks which contain underlying consistencies. Besides, what does he know of classroom gimmicks? He tries to talk with teachers; tries to gather classroom gimmicks; tries to talk with school administrators, convince them that the Project is not just another "expert's" gimmick; runs to his own research project—Floyd the Freireista; learns from Floyd of some of the ideological dangers in the things he preaches on Saturday mornings; tries to publish; tries to be a parent, a husband; tries to stay a step ahead of the guy with the wrench who will cut off the gas or the water or some other utility: and

> Things fall apart; the centre cannot hold;
> Mere anarchy is loosed upon the world.

Yeats describing the plight of modern life. This is Victor in the postmodern world: the institution demanding more for its money, more publications, more students, more service, more; yet little comfort, since there must be two incomes, less than two children, a fragmented family. These are the demands of the middle class. He thought it was like on *Leave It to Beaver.* Maybe it was, once. Not now. Then there is color to contend with.

There is the foreignness of his fellow academics, a fellowship he doesn't feel he belongs in, unpublished, not knowing of procedures and standards, their not appreciating the distances someone of color must travel, telling of hard times when he tries to speak of poverty, telling of that economic bad flu when he speaks of a chronic condition. He is scared, professionally alone, trying to meet all of the profession's demands and his culture's demands to be an active parent, still trying to cope with poverty. And there is no more rainbow, the pot of gold that was to come with the doctorate. Dr. V the Deadbeat. Better to live on welfare in Seattle, among friends, refigure, try to make the dissertation worth something other than continual feelings of failure. The decision is made: on to Channing's basement.

Then a call the day after his decision. Professor Crowley, the first person he had ever read who had written of the sophists—a bigshot. She asks if he'd be interested in Northern Arizona, Flagstaff, says that it's something like the Pacific Northwest but without the rain. He thought Arizona was the desert. A news item in the Independence newspaper: thirty inches of snow in Flagstaff, in March. He visits and is unable to find fault. He will try again.

VII Intellectuals and Hegemony

A long dinner table at a fancy Italian restaurant in New York. Some of Victor's fellow graduate students are seated there. Some of his heroes are seated there too, those he had read. One of his heroes tells of the need for more work on basic writers. Then some glasses of wine later, the same hero tells of being bilked by a portorican boy during the most recent New York City blackout: "Clever, the things these portoricans will do for a buck." The hero seems genuinely charmed by the incident. The comment is completely innocuous. The hero seems not to hear his own stereotyping, seems not to understand, or be troubled by, the economic and racial conditions that make for clever portorican hustlers. And, in his stereotyping, the hero had not seen Victor as a portorican, wouldn't have thought about it, likely, since portoricans are not rhetoricians or compositionists. In the fifteen years since Victor first entered the University, the seven years active as a professional, he has yet to meet another Puerto Rican Professor of Rhetoric and Composition.

The chair of a national organization on composition studies, an African American woman that year, gives Dr. V a call. She calls to warn him that his candidacy for a committee position has been questioned—to her—on the grounds that the seven-seat committee already has three minorities on it. The committee threatened to have representation rather than tokenism. The committee's charge is to review and comment on manuscripts submitted for publication. He reads like never before, more careful than ever before, at pains to demonstrate his thorough understanding of rhetoric, composition, literacy, philosophy—his competence despite his color.

A discussion at the microphones of an open meeting at a professional conference. At issue is divestiture of investments in South Africa. There is an argument that the organization cannot know with certainty which investments are indirectly linked to South Africa. The African American constituency is irate and insistent. Another hero turns to him and asks, "Do you know what they're so upset about?" Victor is struck dumb.

It should be obvious—apartheid. Divestiture does take place, but only after heated debate.

Another conference, another debate. Yet another hero takes the microphone. The hero advises the voting body to act cautiously, says that the organization has taken precipitous actions in times past because it has been unwilling to confront a certain small but very vocal constituency—a thinly veiled reference to the African American membership.

A local hiring committee for a new department chair. Only a handful of the applicants appear to be of color. One makes the final cut, a Latino, minimally qualified, but Affirmative Action must be appeased. Prior to the telephone interview, a member of the committee cautions the rest of the committee, says something like, "We've got to keep an eye out for these people. They've gotten so much handed to them that they might not know their own limitations." Tokenism, not competence, is assumed.

Victor has a private conversation with a boss. Victor talks of the insecurity that comes with the realization that tokenism is rampant. He has seen committee decisions on the basis of a person's race or ethnicity, with little regard to abilities. He knows that one reason he sits on so many committees is because the system is not yet working, that there is too limited a racial or ethnic pool from which to draw. He is glad to take part, figures he has something to offer, realizes that tokenism does serve a purpose to persons of color, the foot in the door, the possibility for opening the door wide for others of color to enter, the possibility for true equity sometime in the future, as the majority learns that people of color are in many ways, especially professionally, no different from whites, equally committed, equally concerned, equally competent, equal at worst. But he can never be sure, not really, of his own competence, can never be sure if the laurels proffered are more honorary for the colored kid than earned. The assurance comes back: "Look, we got the best of both worlds. We filled our quota and got somebody really good to boot." He hears that color was the first consideration.

These scenes, a few among many over the years, are not intended to call any individuals or any organizations or any institutions racist. I believe that all are fundamentally concerned with bettering conditions for people of color and of poverty. Their efforts attest to that. I offer these scenes to demonstrate how deeply embedded racism is, *systemically.* I offer these scenes to suggest the limitations of liberalism, the ideology that has at its base the belief that change is an individual concern, a matter of pulling one's self up by the bootstraps, that all that is needed is to provide the conditions that will facilitate the pull, enough elbow room. It is America's dominant ideology.

Liberalism as an ideology, more than as a political affiliation, is pervasive and extreme. It has taken a radical dimension, a point in which collectivities of any sort must perforce become secondary, the needs of the one surpassing the needs of any other one, a "radical individualism" (LeFevre). The liberal ideology of individualism allows for the unchecked continuance of the bootstrap sensibility. It allows for things like English Only legislation, forced elbow room. It allows for the confusion between immigrant and minority, an ahistorical perspective which doesn't make for seeing how long some groups have been without boots. Even when some within those groups manage to put on boots, the boots are not of the same quality as others' boots, the legacy of internal colonialism. Individualism alone allows Floyd's students to reject a collective sensibility, allows those who are of color, like the students in the traditional freshman composition class of my first research study—like me—to attempt to deny or to downplay our races or cultures or class affiliations in the name of individual achievement. It allows for ascribing certain written conventions with an inherent, universal superiority. For all that, there is, I believe, a collective possibility in America's democratic ideals. But such ideals are too easily countered by the ideology of liberalism, countered by economic forces, countered by the current hegemony. Individuals do need encouragement, but that encouragement needs to be balanced by a recognition of, and a change in, the conditions that effect us all. My boots are on. But they pinch.

Change is possible, I believe. Language used consciously, a matter of rhetoric, is a principal means—perhaps *the* means—by which change can begin to take place. The rhetorical includes writing, a means of learning, of discovery; it includes literature, the discoveries of others. Rhetoric, after all, is how ideologies are carried, how hegemonies are maintained. Rhetoric, then, would be the means by which hegemonies could be countered. And the classroom is an ideal site in which to affect change; the classroom, where we come in contact with so many, the many who in turn will come in contact with many more. It's a utopian hope, but it is the utopian possibility that makes for a teacher. The utopian, I know, drives me, even when tempered by the practical. The problem that makes for the scenes above and the scenes all through this book are in how the utopian is defined, the hegemony which limits how deeply we look.

To change the current hegemony requires an understanding of hegemony. It's a term of some currency, but rarely defined. It's thick, difficult. But it's worth the effort for me, given the possibilities the understanding can provide. To understand hegemony's workings better, we must meet Antonio Gramsci.

To tell of Antonio Gramsci is to tell of a life dramatically affected by the hegemonic forces he sought to oppose. Born among the southern Italian peasantry of Sardinia in 1891, he was the fourth of seven children; a mother, house-bound though literate, from a family of peasants and minor civil servants; a father from the Italian mainland, a civil servant for a local Sardinian registrar's office, a job lost when he opposed a local political figure's bid for election, accused of embezzlement, arrested, released six years later, unemployable.

Antonio drops out of the fifth grade to help the family after his father's arrest. He works ten-hour days, a sickly child, a hunchback since he was six, after having been accidentally dropped down a flight of stairs. He would appear a dwarf-like hunchback in later years.

After years of lugging register books heavier than he, Gramsci returns to school. He attends the *gymnasium* (secondary school), then the *liceo,* then college on a scholarship slotted for the peasantry of promise. At the University of Turin he studies linguistics and classics. Yet illness continually interrupts schooling. He quits, finds work as a journalist.

He writes for a number of radical newspapers. In 1919, he joins three friends in founding *L'Ordine Nuovo,* a paper intended to further the political education of automobile-factory workers at Turin, the home of Fiat, Gramsci's home until his own imprisonment. In 1921, Gramsci leaves *L'Ordine Nuovo* and its sponsor, the Italian Socialist Party. He helps form the Italian Communist Party. Gramsci becomes a central committee member, travels to Moscow, marries Giulia Schuct in 1923. She is a Muscovite of Austrian heritage. Antonio and Giulia have two sons, one which Antonio will never see, the other to be known by Antonio only while it is still a baby. Antonio travels to Vienna and to Lyons, corresponds with Trotsky. Gramsci is a Leninist, a critical one, but a Leninist. Later, in prison, he becomes truly a Gramscian.

While Gramsci travels Russia and France and Italy, a colleague, a former fellow Socialist, Benito Mussolini, gains power. Gramsci is critical of fascism in his writing and speaking tours but does not remain away from Italy. In 1926, while Gramsci is in Rome, he is arrested. Back in 1921, Mussolini had said Gramsci had "an unquestionably powerful brain" (Entwistle 8). So in 1928 Mussolini proclaims, by way of the public prosecutor, that "for twenty years we must stop this brain from functioning" (*Notebooks* lxxxix). The brain hardly stops. Nine years later, 1937, Gramsci dies in a prison hospital, a victim of the western world's first fascist regime.

From peasantry to prison, Gramsci's thinking goes through four discernable intellectual phases, not a linear intellectual evolution, really, yet each phase effecting what will become the *Prison Notebooks.* The first phase, 1914–1919, finds Gramsci a neo-Hegelian, following Benedetto Croce, Italy's most noted philosopher. Gramsci writes of worker's revolutionary *spirit;* the spiritual is a Hegelian idea. From 1919–1920, during Italy's *biennio rosso* (The Red Years), a period of massive worker revolts, Gramsci becomes more the Marxist: considerations of economics. He writes of class consciousness arising within factory councils (*consigli di fabbrica*). He writes of imminent revolution. The council movement collapses. From 1921–1926, Gramsci the Bolshevik: belief in Lenin's revolutionary vanguard elite, great political activity, but no great theoretical activity. The final phase, 1929–1935, marks most of Gramsci's prison years. He fills thirty-two notebooks, over 2,800 pages (nearly 4,000 typed). He develops his understanding of hegemony, his considerations of intellectuals, the historical bloc, war of positions, and other matters. These are the *Prison Notebooks,* what Perry Anderson has called the greatest work in the Western Marxist tradition (54).

Gramsci believes "Concrete experience is the essential material of human reflection . . . the products of this reflection then proceed[ing] to modify the social reality from which they emerge" (Femia 132). Gramsci's experiences would lead to his repudiation of Croce (though not humanism), to subjectivity, an idealist strain. Lenin would be lauded, credited with the concept of hegemony, but Lenin would be virtually theorized out of Gramsci's conception of hegemony. Marxism would be stripped of its scientism. The linguistics of his university years would remain. He would break new ground.

Hegemony is the ground's breaker. The usual definition: hegemony equals ideological domination. Gramsci adds an essential qualifier: domination by consent. Without consent, hegemony fails. And consent is granted ideologically. As Gramsci sees it, every culture contains particular worldviews, ideologies; some of these are common to the cultures within a society and are common to the cultures that comprise the dominant groups. We accept commonly held worldviews as truths. The dominant does more than accept; it capitalizes. We accept the dominant's actions as based on truths; we approve of acts based on truths; we consent.

Too dense. I'll thin it out some.

Hegemony contains a variety of ideologies. Some of these ideologies are artificial. They are theoretical constructs, though not necessarily created by the dominant groups. Artificial ideologies might be constructed by political activists, like the leaders of revolutionary parties, for instance, or by academics. The ideological constructs turn out to be descriptive, but abstract, more like explanations than lived experiences. This is the stuff of a graduate course on literary critical theory since 1965 or of a graduate political-science course—of esoteric academic journals, mainly. Gramsci terms these "philosophical ideologies." Insofar as they are theoretical descriptions, they are linguistic.

Other ideologies are organic. Gramsci calls these the "common sense." The common sense consists of the commonly held conceptions of the world held by various cultures, a culture's ways of seeing and believing. These are carried and transmitted by discourse. "[L]anguage = thought," writes Gramsci (*Cultural Writings* 129), and "every language contains the elements of a conception of the world" (Gramsci, *Materialismo storico,* quoted in Femia 44). Language is epistemic, says Gramsci; the episteme contains ideology. These are new ideas, discussed by Gramsci a half century before they become new.

Hegemony exploits language and the worldview it contains, making for something like the rhetorician Kenneth Burke's "ultimate terms." If reality, or at least a view of reality, a worldview, is linguistically defined, then alternatives to that reality in the absence of alternative terms becomes a problem. Accept "democracy" as a "God term" (to borrow from another rhetorician, Richard Weaver) and reject "socialism" or "Marxism" as a "devil term," and no term comes to mind during times when democracy breaks down. There is discomfort, but no language with which to explain the discomfort. In the absence of alternate terms, reform might be sought and accepted, but substantive, revolutionary change remains virtually unthinkable. Consent is not withdrawn. Hegemony is maintained.

Hegemony survives by its sensitivity to changes in cultures' conceptions. Hegemony watches over and works with changes in language. "Colonialism" might lose favor in common sense, but the need for dominance remains. Political theorists might claim "neo-colonialism," but the operant term of the dominant becomes "national economic security"; common sense rallies accordingly, not quite ready to relinquish an imperial past. Common sense changes but still holds elements of older ways. That is, common sense maintains elements of previous hegemonies, reflecting current forces while containing previous forces, reflecting past ideologies and ideological struggles as well as present ones, reflecting past social relations and current relations. Common sense turns out to be varied, "disjointed and episodic" (Gramsci, *Materialismo storico,* quoted in Femia 45), even contradictory.

The ideological elements which are necessary to hegemony must be maintained and passed on, reproduced. The institutions which pass on common sense and thereby serve the dominant hegemony are found within "civil society." Civil society, as Gramsci defines it, is "the ensemble of organisms commonly called 'private' [which] . . . correspond[s] . . . to the function of 'hegemony' which the dominant group exercises throughout society" (*Notebooks* 12). In other words, civil society consists of culture's institutions: things like family, religion, education, the media. Through these organisms, civil society endorses the ethical beliefs and manners which maintain hegemony.

Consider the workings of the early church and popular political ideology in America, for instance. Gramsci writes of America as having an unusually well-integrated hegemony because of its short history. Early settlers could discard their links to past ideologies—the monarchy, the nobility of the feudal system, the feudal peasantry. America's founders, writes Gramsci, were the

> protagonists of the political and religious struggles in England, defeated but not humiliated or laid low in their country of origin. They import into America . . . apart from moral energy and energy of the will, a certain stage of European historical evolution, which, when transplanted by such men into the virgin soil of America, continues to develop the forces implicit in its nature but with incomparably more rapid rhythms than in Old Europe, where there exists a whole series of checks (moral, intellectual, political, economic) incorporated in specific sections of the population, relics of past regimes which refuse to die out, which generate opposition to speedy progress and give to every initiative the equilibrium of mediocrity, diluting it in time and space. (*Notebooks* 20)

In other words, the new society would be unencumbered by the slowing elements of long-established and long-lived traditions and thereby move forward at great speed. Then the settlers' dominant religion's work ethic supports capitalism: shoulder to the wheel, a penny saved is a penny earned, waste not want not, self-discipline, thrift, hard work. Liberal politics, with its emphasis on individualism and *laissez-faire* economics, transmitted through the pulpit, the press, town-hall meetings, further serves capitalists (owners of the means of production, the bourgeoisie).

These same ingredients become the yeast in the rise of corporate economy. Efficiency and pride in *things* produced becomes pride in *pay* produced. Gramsci calls this hegemonic shift "a psycho-physical adaptation to the new industrial structure, aimed for through high wages" (*Notebooks* 286). Individual responsibility in puritanism, individual achievement in liberal politics, an economic system which has only known capitalism—all of this makes for a memory which knows of no other social constructions, no other forms of government, no other means of production. Americans can't think of a different way to do things because America has never known different ways of doing things. Hegemony in America is virtually watertight—and thereby relatively easy to pass on through civil society.

Hegemony is virtually watertight here, but not quite. There is leakage, most often caused by those who have been traditionally excluded from the bounties of the dominant hegemony. So hegemony must account for those whose common sense contains memories different from those of the early settlers. Hegemony must shift.

Sometimes the shifts seem radical. Gramsci calls seemingly radical hegemonic shifts "passive revolution" or "revolution-restoration." Civil rights protests lead to affirmative action. People of color and women are granted greater access to America's bounties. But there are no structural changes that would remove basic inequities, no "concrete revolution." And the changes are accepted. Revolution-restoration or passive revolution (pacifying revolution, more like) is not accepted because people are unaware of exploitation. We're aware. We know. We know that others gain wealth and power at the expense of our labors. We know, but we accept. Acceptance is a form of consent.

We accept because self-interest prevails. As long as interests are met, and as long as general senses of morality and ethics are assuaged, consent continues to be granted. Hegemony survives.

Something more than simple reform is possible, however. There is counter hegemony: a matter of individual and collective will—and active rhetorical practice. Scientific Marxism in Gramsci's time held that conditions would arise which would precipitate the forceful inculcation of change: the economy would crash; the workers would revolt. But Gramsci had seen economic crashes without subsequent revolutions. No "natural" evolution toward revolution. Although Gramsci would not discount armed conflict, a "war of maneuver," he saw armed conflict as secondary, to be preceded by a long "war of position," a counter hegemony.

Gramsci recognized that advanced capitalism, when coupled with imperialism, would make for unprecedented cultural and ideological diversity within civil society and would make for a decidedly strong State. The State is strong when the people are fragmented. The divided are easily conquered. The greater the empire, the greater the fragmentation because of many peoples. But the State would remain ideologically unified, having a concentrated military and economic control. There would be too many fragments to congeal as a unified force against the concentrated power of the State. This is a pretty accurate picture of contemporary America. But what makes a war of maneuver all the more unlikely for America is America's unusually well-knit hegemony. Whatever the contradictions, whatever the current economy, there is movement within and through the classes; there is still affluence for many and the belief in the possibility for affluence within the current system for many more—though the rising discontent and its manifestations in violence in the ghettos suggest that the belief in future possibility is dwindling. So there will be changes in Los Angeles, the Southside of Chicago, Detroit, Bed-Stuy, enough to quiet the discontent for a time.

America has a special talent for revolution-restoration, is able to keep hope alive. It has to be good at making adjustments. America *must* operate on consent. It must maintain a kind of democracy, even as it continues to make decisions without consulting its people. So here's a thought: if America's great numbers were to withdraw consent, would dominant groups lose their grip without turning to armed retaliation? Maybe. There is at least the possibility that a war of position would be sufficient to inculcating substantive change (Adamson 226).

A war of position is waged rhetorically. Gramsci tells of crises which give rise to a war of position: a conjunctural crisis or an organic crisis. A conjunctural crisis occurs when there is general, deep-rooted dissatisfaction with leadership. It is immediate. Voices are loud, antagonistic. Three possible outcomes come of the conjunctural. "Political society" can react. Political society is the coercive arm of the State. I think of the police riots at the Chicago Democratic convention, or the National Guard at Kent State, the FBI against the Black Panther Party. Another possible outcome would be revolution-restoration. Voices speaking out against McCarthyism make for greater intellectual freedom, with socialist activism being handled ideologically: talk of communist-bloc nations repudiating socialism, say, failing to mention that those nations were more statist-bureaucratic than socialist. Watergate: voices speak out; Nixon resigns; a few others are sentenced to white-collar prisons; and the general political situation returns to normal. The other possibility is that the conjunctural can become organic.

Organic crisis occurs when there is widespread socio-historical criticism. Voices of discontent look back to the roots of oppression and articulate the socio-historical precedents. This is Floyd's re-creation of history. America may be in the midst of an organic crisis right now, as more people seek to remedy the causes of basic inequity. Civil rights and women's rights have had conjunctural moments, when voices have shouted. Both the civil rights movement and the women's movement have been met with revolution-restoration through affirmative action and the like. Civil rights and the women's movement have been confronted by political society: turns in abortion laws, outright armed confrontation against organized African Americans, English Only laws. Yet the fundamental changes sought by both women and people of color are still being articulated. But the leadership's voices are softer now, for the most part, seeking, in Burke's term, identification with the other groups within civil society. Voices are more "academic," laying out the historical bases for discontent, explaining the pressures exerted on all of society by the long-term oppression of some. The voices seek to persuade all groups that everyone's needs could be better met if substantive changes were to take place. And this is true.

In other words, an organic strategy within a war of position seeks to bring about a new hegemony. For Gramsci, this means forming a new "historic bloc." An historic bloc is formed when a war of position has been so successful that changes are sought and brought into effect throughout the cultural, political, and economic sectors of society.

This is something less than armed revolution; something more than reform.

A new consensus is formed—a new hegemony. Consent, the key to hegemony, has to be gained through careful articulation and negotiation throughout the social system.

New terms, or new definitions for existing terms, agreeable to all, have to be developed. "Socialized medicine" becomes "national health insurance," for instance. The war of position underlies Freire's hope, that in changing the word we would change the world (Freire and Macedo).

An historic bloc, formed by a war of position, in order to bring about a new hegemony is, then, brought about by persuasive articulatory practice.

Hegemony is rhetorical.

The principal agent in countering the current hegemony (or in conserving it, for that matter; but more on this below) is the intellectual—a "permanent persuader," in Gramsci's words (*Notebooks* 10).

The intellectual actively seeking substantive social change is a rhetor. But she is not necessarily an academic or someone employed to perform mental labor; "intellectual" has a broader meaning for Gramsci. Everyone is potentially an intellectual: "All men [and all women] are intellectuals . . . but not all men [nor all women] have in society the function of intellectuals," writes Gramsci. We are—all of us—workers *and* intellectuals: "*homo faber* cannot be separated from *homo sapiens*" (*Notebooks* 9). Yet Gramsci does describe those who have "the function of intellectuals."

Among those who do intellectual work, there are traditional intellectuals and organic intellectuals. At times Gramsci suggests that organic intellectuals are only those who remain intimately tied to the organizations which are part of their class or group, like a Cesar Chavez. At other times, Gramsci describes organic intellectuals as those whose work remains tied to the classes from which they originated, even if they work outside their original communities. That is, organic intellectuals might function within more traditional intellectual organizations, like the university, yet remain organic if the functions they undertake have them conceptualizing and articulating the social, economic, and political interests of the group or class from which they came.

Organic intellectuals are involved in a dialectical and rhetorical enterprise: reliance on personal experiences and the experiences of the groups from which they came in order to attract other groups, including traditional intellectuals. When the organic intellectual is involved in this enterprise she becomes Gramsci's "new intellectual." She becomes a "permanent persuader," involved "in active participation in practical life, as constructor, organizer" (*Notebooks* 10). She acts as an intellectual liaison between the groups seeking revolutionary change and the rest of civil society.

Gramsci approaches traditional intellectuals two ways: historically and ideologically. Historically, traditional intellectuals are those who might have been organic at one time but lost their links to the organizations they once represented. The best example for Gramsci (coming from Catholic Italy) is the ecclesiast. The ecclesiast (and others, like artists, writers, some philosophers) might have been born of the feudal system, but managed to survive the demise of the system. They managed to survive through an idealist ideology which masked their separation from the means of production. Having survived their original allegiances, traditional intellectuals come to believe that they transcend social-class groupings, that they stand apart from the exigencies of socio-political change. In Italy, the Church absorbed the intellectual;

in France and England, clerics (and the aristocracy) were economically absorbed by the bourgeoisie. Traditional intellectuals, believing themselves autonomous, unwittingly become "the dominant group's 'deputies' exercising the subaltern functions of social hegemony and political government" (*Notebooks* 12). In other words, traditional intellectuals pass on the "truths" of the State and the dominant hegemony in their work within subaltern institutions, the institutions of civil society.

The traditional intellectual is no less the servant of the current hegemony in Gramsci's more ideological descriptions. Traditional intellectuals, even those who are conscious of class relations, are subject to a "directive hegemony," an element of hegemony which seeks to control. Gramsci describes two ways in which a directive hegemony operates over intellectuals. One way is through an insistence on specialization. Intellectuals are enjoined to have "an activity of their own in their technical field," keeping them tightly focused on minutiae, keeping them from contemplating the "ensemble of relations" (*Notebooks* 104). Academics, for instance, are subject to accelerated publish-or-perish rates in specific, specialized journals. Or academics can be pressured into seeking research funding, with grants foundations insisting on "pure theory" or "pure research," keeping them from active participation in social matters.

The other way a directive hegemony exerts influence is by allowing, in Gramsci's words, "a general conception of life, a philosophy . . . which offers to its adherents an intellectual 'dignity' providing a principle of differentiation from the old ideologies which dominated by coercion, and an element of struggle against them" (*Notebooks* 103–14). Simply put, intellectuals are allowed a degree of dissent. I think of intellectual Marxism, which, whatever its insights, is rendered harmless by its "academicity": its exclusive language, gibberish to all but other academic intellectual Marxists. Theirs is an arhetorical dissent. I think of Louis Althusser, his insightful descriptions of ideological oppression from the State—and his seeing himself as a "theoricist," above class struggles. He dissents, yet holds onto the traditional notion that as an intellectual he is autonomous. Traditional intellectuals remain distanced from organic intellectuals and the populace at large. In effect, they remain tied to hegemony.

Gramsci also specifically addresses American intellectuals. For Gramsci, all American intellectuals are organic intellectuals. There are no American traditional intellectuals because of America's "lack of [the kind of] sedimentation . . . one finds in countries of ancient civilizations" (*Notebooks* 20). Without conceptions drawn from a feudal past, the American intellectual provides an organic intellectual's function of articulating the interests of more than an elite few. The American intellectual's organic task, according to Gramsci, is in formulating a uniquely American history, thereby helping to create a single, unifying national culture that would include "the different forms of culture imported by immigrants of differing national origins" (*Notebooks* 20). For Gramsci, a national culture is a necessary precondition for creating a counter hegemony.

But I believe that now, more than a half century after Gramsci's writing, intellectuals who follow Gramsci's role for the American intellectual would be doing more to maintain than to counter hegemony. America now does have its traditional intellectuals. Although the national culture has to great extent included "immigrants of different national origins," it has not included all who are Americans in the same way. Internal colonialism remains. We now recognize, in a way that Gramsci would not have, that there are groups in America whose origins are different from immigrants, groups who have been part of America from its inception. There are the American Indians, obviously, already in America when the pilgrims arrived, when the pioneers explored. Women were pilgrims, were pioneers, standing alongside the men. The founding fathers brought their slaves. Spaniards preceded the British founders and were later incorporated into America as America expanded. A national culture having only immigrants in mind threatens to maintain the status quo. Maintaining the status quo is the function—even when unintended—of traditional intellectuals.

America's minorities are closer to Gramsci's peasantry than to immigrants (America's farmers more like an economically depressed petty bourgeoisie). Gramsci describes the peasantry as having become victims of a particular ideology which described their "organic inca-pacity... their barbarity, their biological inferiority. These already wide-spread opinions," writes Gramsci, "were consolidated and actually theorized by the sociologists of positivism ... acquiring the strength of 'scientific truth' in a period of superstition about science" (*Notebooks* 71).

America has known a similar trend. America has known Jensen on the genetic inferiority of African Americans, Madison Grant on the cultural inferiority of "new immigrants," the inferiority of Latinos, Mexican Americans. America has known Bereiter's verbal-deficit theory, Farrell's oral-culture hypothesis. America has had its positivists proving the "organic incapacity... barbarity, ... biological inferiority" of its version of the peasantry long after Gramsci had declared that this is what is done, long after he had written about how it's done. Gramsci's notion that a national culture would allow all people to partake in a counter hegemony does not apply in America if the national culture is to be obtained through a melting-pot sensibility. Some of us have been traditionally kept from melting, even those whose great ambition was to melt.

American traditional intellectuals are holdovers from the melting-pot sensibility. They are analogous to Gramsci's traditional intellectuals as the holdovers from the feudal sensibility. The American traditional intellectual, like Gramsci's ideological description of traditional intellectuals, perform functions "which are not all justified by the social necessities of production, though they are justified by the political necessities of the dominant fundamental group" (*Notebooks* 13). We continue to hear of the melting pot, but we also continue to hear of the inordinately small numbers of women and minorities at the highest ranks of corporate structures, the seats of real hegemonic power. Despite the historical differences between European and American intellectuals, America does have its traditional intellectuals.

Now, if these various distinctions among intellectuals seem confusing it is because they are confused in Gramsci, who was never to revise, never to organize or to unify his ideas in the *Prison Notebooks*. For the sake of convenience, then, let me simplify the distinctions among intellectuals. Organic intellectuals: representatives of the groups from which they come, not the dominant. Traditional intellectuals: servants of the dominant hegemony. New intellectuals: the ideal, a fusion of organic and traditional, actively engaged in the rhetorical enterprise of a counter hegemony.

It is possible for the would-be new intellectual to function as a traditional intellectual, given particular ideological assumptions. E. D. Hirsch provides an extreme example. I'm not saying that Hirsch's educational scheme is subversive, of course, that he is a new intellectual. I am saying that Hirsch means well, is interested in change. Hirsch advocates a national culture, a good thing according to Gramsci (but more on this later). Hirsch is "committed to pluralism" (*Cultural Literacy* 95). Hirsch is surely rhetorical—a persuader, the principal attribute of the new intellectual. As a persuader, Hirsch's ethos in *Cultural Literacy* displays the charming intellectual: calling on authorities from Plato to Rousseau to Dewey, science from standardized tests to schema theory to social theory, references from women in high places like Jeanne Chall, African Americans at Harvard or in the Black Panther Party, anecdotes from his father, the merchant, to his son, the school teacher. He has won the ear of a large portion of the American public. He is obviously persuasive, given bestseller status and a successful cultural literacy dictionary.

Hirsch fits Gramsci's description of the American intellectual. Richard Ohmann, whose *Politics of Letters* shows his understanding of Gramsci on intellectuals, sees Hirsch as an organic intellectual (organically tied to the class in power ("Graduate Students" 256). This works if we don't modify Gramsci, if we accept that there are no traditional American intellectuals. But, like I said, I believe there are. And I believe Hirsch is one—an example of the American brand of the traditional intellectual.

I'll skip a detailed critique of Hirsch's cultural literacy. Others do that well enough. And as I mentioned in the previous chapter, I'm not quite ready to throw the whole concept out, despite its problems. For now, however, I would like to focus on one ideological aspect: Hirsch's perception of the American middle class. His perception of the middle class is likely shared by many who would have America be more equitably representative of its citizenry, many would-be new intellectuals.

Hirsch claims that national cultures and national languages transcend ideologies (*Cultural Literacy* 82). Because cultural literacy is from the middle class, is used and altered over time by the middle class, it is not elitist, he says. Since it consists of elements from all of America's cultures, it is neither ethnocentric, racist, nor sexist, he says. The middle class, after all, says Hirsch, is the dominant source of the national language and the national culture. He seems to believe that the middle class is the source of American power and the desired goal of all.

But the whole notion of "the middle class" is ideological. Hirsch separates the notion of the middle class from ideology-as-political in a manner described by Karl Marx in *On the Jewish Question,* where Marx is explicitly referring to America. Writes Marx:

> The state abolishes, after its fashion, the distinctions established by *birth, social rank, education, occupation,* when it decrees that birth, social rank, education, occupation are *non-political* distinctions; when it proclaims, without regard to these distinctions, that every member of society is an *equal* partner in popular sovereignty. (Quoted in Tucker 33).

Marx claims that the State propagates the notion of a classless society. Although there are many who still hold to this idea, it has been modified along the lines delineated by Hirsch: not a classless society, but a middle-class society. Gramsci would qualify the idea that the State is directly responsible, since some of these ideas would come out of the common sense. But Gramsci would acknowledge that civil society propagates the notion of a relatively non-political or trans-political unifying entity called "the middle class." Equality within the middle class remains part of common sense, even though we know that women of the middle class do not share equitably with the men of the middle class. The notion remains, even though we know that castelike minorities of the middle class do not enjoy the same bounties as middle-class whites. These are the differences which come together as the notion of internal colonialism. The middle class is even called America's bourgeoisie, though the middle class is not the bourgeoisie in a bourgeois hegemony (America's hegemony). The bourgeoisie are the owners of the means of production—the corporate owners, not even the CEOs.

The middle is not the top. Members of the middle class occupy contradictory locations within the class system (Wright). With some exceptions, members of the middle class are wage earners who exploit others. Corporate executives exploit middle management, middle managers their subordinates, franchise "owners" their employees. Theirs is a pseudo-hegemonic power: hiring and firing, owning corporate stock, making capital investments, accruing property, and so forth. The middle class gets to *feel* like those with substantial socio-political power. But the middle class is not the World Bank, has no control over the International Monetary Fund, is not the bourgeoisie, is not among those who really do manipulate national and international political states. Whatever power the middle class enjoys, it is not substantive hegemonic power. The middle class abides by the overall hegemony.

Cultural literacy succeeds because it appeals to the common sense notion that to achieve middle-class status is to have made it. And cultural literacy receives support (moral and fiscal) because it serves the current hegemony. Hirsch's cultural literacy provides no critical dimension, despite Hirsch's assertion that a national language and a national culture are necessary even for dissension. Even in matters of dissension, Hirsch does not chip at the hegemonic bloc. He refers to the Black Panthers' newspaper, for example. He applauds the Black Panthers' writers on their rigorous education and their use of national-cultural literary allusions in forwarding their revolutionary cause (22–23). Yet he never mentions how the Black Panther Party's war of maneuver was violently overthrown by political society. Hirsch stops short of substantially affecting the status quo.

Cultural literacy provides workers for a post-industrial nation which requires readers and writers. To the extent that the need includes women and people of color, cultural literacy potentially allows everyone access to the middle class and at least the possibility for affluence, if not real power. The truism that money means power does not include the money or the power of the middle class. Money means the possibility for movement more than power, freedom from complete powerlessness more than real power. A curriculum that conceives of empowerment as enabling access to the middle class is fundamentally traditional, no matter the doffs of the hat to women's studies, minority literature, multiculturalism. At bottom, there is still hegemony.

Yet it is true that there are similarities between Hirsch's educational scheme and Gramsci's. Gramsci, like Hirsch, would foster the creation of a national culture. Gramsci advocates instruction in *haute couture:* Greco-Roman traditions, the Renaissance, art, the theater, literature. He advocates the creation of a standard national language.

Gramsci would have his reasons. Gramsci's Italy had an inordinate number of regional dialects. Some dialects were so different as to constitute nearly different languages. Although there had been legislated attempts at imparting a national Italian, the attempts had failed because poverty made for poor school attendance and because language instruction, as far as Gramsci was concerned, had little to do with language. Emphasis was placed on grammar instruction. Since Gramsci believes language is thought, and thereby contains culturally specific ideological conceptions, the lack of a national standard language would maintain a fragmented society. Subalterns would not be able to enter into the kinds of rhetorical practices that would make for the unity necessary to a counter hegemony. A national language would be necessary in articulating a working-class ethos.

The working classes would also need to formulate their own culture ("culture" in the sense of philosophy and the arts). Instruction in the existing arts would define and demonstrate what constitutes the cultured. Gramsci goes so far as to insist that education include a thorough understanding of the rights and duties of citizenry as professed by the State. But such an education is to be presented in a manner "which challenges the conceptions that are imparted by the various traditional social environments, i.e., those conceptions which can be termed folkloristic" (*Notebooks* 30). At this juncture, Hirsch and Gramsci part ways.

According to Gramsci, all education should include the folkloristic:

> Folklore should . . . be studied as a "conception of the world and life" implicit to a large extent in determinate (in time and space) strata of society and in opposition (also for the most part implicit, mechanical and objective) to "official" conceptions of the world (or in a broader sense, the conceptions of the cultured parts of

historically determinate societies) that have succeeded one another
in the historical process. (*Cultural Writings* 189)

In short, education in traditions and in a national language should be
placed in historical perspective such that ideologies and mythologies
would be exposed. This would include "modern folklore": philosophy
and science. Gramsci observed "that certain opinions and scientific
notions, removed from their context and more or less distorted,
constantly fall within the popular domain and are 'inserted' into the
mosaic of tradition" (*Cultural Writings* 189). Even if philosophy and
science aim at the objective or the universal, they are nevertheless
conscripted into the service of hegemony. Exposing modern folklore
would likely fall on those involved in science and philosophy, academics.

Those who comprise the various cultures within the classroom would
be encouraged to discover their own folklore. A national language and
a national culture might be imparted through traditional educational
means, like straight lecture, but the critical aspects implicit in the
folkloristic would make for a classroom, in Gramsci's words, "in which
everybody participates, to which everybody contributes, in which everybody is both master and disciple" (*Cultural Writings* 25). Gramsci's
educational scheme is both Hirsch's *and* Paulo Freire's. Gramsci's
scheme is rhetorical: providing for a dialectic among students, a dialectic
between student and teacher, between lived experiences and official
ideologies. Gramsci's educational scheme amounts to a *critical* cultural
literacy.

Hegemony is shifting. A telltale sign of the shift can be found in
the political push for universal literacy. Writes Gramsci:

> Each time that in one way or another, the question of language
> comes to the fore, that signifies that a series of other problems is
> about to emerge, the formation and enlarging of the ruling class,
> the necessity to establish more "intimate" and sure relations
> between the ruling groups and the national popular masses, that
> is, the reorganization of cultural hegemony. (*Cultural Writings*
> 183–84)

The current great interest in literacy coincides with the economy's shift
from industry to service, which also coincides with economic crisis.
Those in truly dominant positions need a larger middle-class work
force. They need more mental laborers. So hegemony fosters the
commonsensical notion that mental work is not labor. Rhetorically,
hegemony plays up the blue collar/white collar distinction and down-
plays its hold on both collars' chains. Hegemony also plays up "upward
mobility" as social change. Yet widening the mental-labor pool means

drawing from the now unnecessarily large physical-labor pool. People of color, who have traditionally waded in the physical pool in disproportionate numbers, would surely be drawn into the new pool. In order to have two workers for what had once been the spending power of one, women too must be drawn into the middle-class pool. Media tell of the advancements fostered by the women's movement (not necessarily feminism). Yet the media, part of civil society, confines its discussions of advancement to discussions of women in the work force, leaving relatively alone questions of substantive ideological or political advancement among women. The same is also true when it comes to people of color. The changes we see taking place are too strikingly commensurate with changing needs within the current hegemony.

The changes can be turned to counter-hegemonic advantage, however. Changing demographics make for classrooms filled with the children of color, those whose common sense likely differs from the white middle class. The current changes in the dominant's needs also make for a greater entry into the universities of those who have been traditionally excluded. It may well be that those who enter the universities come with the hegemonic common sense, for the most part, since they wouldn't be likely to be in the universities otherwise. But their "sedimentation," their memories of an older common sense, would be different from more traditional university students. The traditionally excluded might better see the contradictions in the current hegemony. The existence of more readily apparent contradictions has counter-hegemonic possibilities. The same applies to the other grades, where the needs for literacy education can be turned to counter-hegemonic advantage in the combination of the cultural with the critical.

By the same token, the new proletarianization, where labor includes the word processor as well as the assembly line, should remind us that we, educators, are no less the new working class. We too wear collars, even if looser than many. American academics can enjoy the social prestige granted to the elite but suffer the economic status of the rest. Academics enjoy a great deal of latitude in going about their work, but are nevertheless wage earners, subject to bureaucratic controls; no punch clocks or requirements to stay at the office, but long work days and nights nevertheless.

American academics are necessarily subject to a directive hegemony—even when pursuing organic functions. Economic necessity, at the very least (keeping a job, gaining tenure, getting promoted), guarantees a degree of compliance. No matter our good intentions, we are pulled by contradictory forces—the hegemonic against the subversive (Boggs 287).

In essential, hegemonic terms, we are no different from our students. As our status as workers becomes more apparent and as we come more in contact with more of those who are intellectuals from non-traditional backgrounds, we find ourselves in a potentially decisive moment. The moment is right for America's intellectuals in traditional academic roles to help organic intellectuals recognize themselves as such and to begin to fuse with them—creating Gramsci's new intellectuals.

This is not to say that we would convert our classrooms into political propaganda pits. The war of position is a protracted war. Hegemony will not be countered in one semester or in one quarter or two. We cannot deny students' economic desires nor our own economic needs. But we can begin the dialectical process necessary to a counter hegemony. We can play out our contradictions as deputies of hegemony and as subversives, agents of tradition and, with our students, potential agents of change. We can follow Gramsci's example: promoting critical dialogue within a cultural literacy. Every classroom practice I have described in previous chapters has kept this in mind.

As the dropout-turned-scholar types the manuscript that will be *Bootstraps,* he has to make yet another summer. Not enough pay to stretch over twelve months. It's that simple, not a matter of excessive spending, excessive consumption, having never qualified for a middle-class plastic passport—a Visa or a MasterCard. Uncertainty is simply his summer lot. He'll qualify for food stamps, get a part-time job as short-order cook for a local greasy spoon. The published college professor, still eligible for state aid despite a state salary. Middle management had denied his request for two summer teaching stints—so that he could get on with his writing. Good intentions, but no grip on the economics of class ascendancy while playing out the contradiction of other-cultural traditions.

He and Carol break hegemonic and economic rules. They would not institutionalize their children. He had done that once and had come to regret it: his son's childhood unretrievable, lost, the boy grown and gone, not even a Christmas call—lost while the now professor was still chasing the carrot. Love and *la sangre* raise children; institutions maintain them. Even if Carol and he would rationalize that there will come the someday when they would be with their kids (while the days pass away relentlessly), Carol is not even worth a minimum wage on the job market, not worth enough to cover child care, according to the marketplace. Two dropouts, two of the poor, two of the traditionally excluded, the colored and the woman. Hegemony's passive revolution does not provide equity, only its semblance. One seeping through the crack in the current hegemony's historic bloc is enough to show the system works.

And then he is subject to a directive hegemony—the institution's ways. No ill will toward middle management. He knows it has his best interests in mind, good intentions. Yet middle management hasn't a clue. They too are walled within the current hegemony. And he hadn't a clue. He thought the Ph.D. would be the end to suffering of this sort—begging for work with dignity and with meaning and being denied, having to return to menial labor, to welfare. To welfare! Stalking about at Safeway at six in the morning so as not to be seen with the food stamps legally tendered, ashamed despite full knowledge of the economics of color, the workings of hegemony.

Then comes fall. It always does. And the economic cycle begins anew. The salary is gone in repairing summer's economic damage, trying to keep the promises made in those demeaning calls to the landlord and the utility companies. And there continues the caring for children, their subsistence needs, their not-to-be-denied needs for Halloween or Christmas or Easter, the birthdays—all magical days, the joys the parents get in providing the joys, but the expenses nevertheless. And then come the ill-afforded trips to conferences, in part because they're necessary to job security; in part because they provide yet another instance of teaching and learning. And economic ascendancy continues to seem so close, the carrot touching lips.

And with fall comes the students. There comes the fun of the performance, expression of the need to pass things on, the learning the students pass on to him, the hope for a better future for all. And he knows again that the suffering is worth something few enjoy: the children and the students provide a life filled with meaning and possibility. He'd rather skip how he's come to know the things he speaks about and writes about, still hankering after a piece of the pie while believing less that there are pieces left, but he knows he could not be who he is, finding pleasure and promise in what he does, without having lived as he has to this point.

A Post(modern)script

This is a postmodern text. It fits no specific genre; its presentation, on the surface, is fragmentary. There is a Foucauldian strain to it: the mixed genres, the narrative disunity, the several selves, the personal history's attempts at analyzing how "mechanisms of power have been— and continue to be—invested, colonized . . . by ever more general mechanisms and by forms of global domination," in Foucault's words (quoted in Harvey 45). There might be a Derridian element: the apparent discontinuity and alinearity facilitating the reader's partici- pation in creating the text. And maybe the text displays a Lacanian schizophrenia. It is surely postmodern to assume that other voices, speaking differently, are to be legitimated. But I'm just playing the postmodern academic's role in saying all this. It may all be true, but not all intended.

It is obvious for those well-versed in poststructuralism that this text is not poststructuralist. The text reflects a belief that there is still a need to speak in terms of a coherent politic, a totality, to use a term by Gyorgy Lukacs, a "global perspective." There is a metanarrative here, a grounding philosophy, a theoretical foundation: Gramsci, Marx- ism, broadly defined. There is a linearity, a hierarchical ordering in which all is intended to congeal in the end, in how all that precedes the final chapter can be placed within the final chapter's Gramscian framework. And that ordering suggests induction, a kind of Aristote- lianism, a modern discourse, even if sophistically, poststructurally, "postmodernically" presented. The text is not quite poststructuralist, but it does reflect the postmodern condition.

The postmodern condition is the unignorable crisis in modernism. Postmodernists are delineating or exploring, quite rightly I would think, the fragmentation, the chaos, the ephemeral which has been the problematic in modernism, the things that just won't gel, or just won't fall into place, or just won't go along with the program—the elements that modernism has sought, unsuccessfully, to transcend through in- ordinate attention to the rational, the scientific, the objective. And the special privilege we proffer to the objective, the scientific, the rational remains, despite the "post-" in postmodernism. Modernism is not yet dead. Hegemony is episodic, containing elements of past hegemonies.

Postmodernism marks nothing more than a hegemonic shift, not quite an altogether new era. Marxism, for instance, is hardly a living dinosaur, breathing its last, being artificially kept alive in university English departments, as some would have it (Hairston). Even Pope John Paul II, hardly a radical, "does not attack Marxism or liberal secularism, *because they are the wave of the future,*" says someone close to the Pope, the theologian Rocco Buttiglione (quoted in Harvey 41, emphasis added). That English departments are only now discussing Marxist notions, deeply embedded elsewhere, only shows the degrees to which English departments, the transmitters of traditions, have been silenced (though this is likely true for Americans generally, Marxism and Soviet Socialism having been so thoroughly intermeshed in the American mind, most visibly through McCarthy). There is a Marxism to postmodernity; there is post-Marxism, alive and well in the social sciences, for example, and its language is more and more expressed in Gramscian terms (see Nelson and Grossberg).

But I don't mean to defend Marxism, certainly not to defend modernism. I mention them mainly to demonstrate the danger in facile labeling—modern, postmodern, Marxist, Aristotelian. My more immediate intention is to attempt to avoid a ghettoizing of this text, to avoid its labeling as simply the story of a person of color, to avoid its being read as yet another fragment. There are several labels that might be derived from the title and the text: (1) bootstraps as a reference to the ideology of radical individualism, (2) of color, (3) an academic, (4) an American. The text is, it is true, the voice of an American of color, a representation of people of color to the degree that representation is at all possible. It is also the voice of an academic, carrying with it some very traditional academic ways. And it is the voice of an American.

The problems of the American of color are real. Ghettos are growing larger, not smaller. Racism seems more entrenched than ever, a condition that arises whenever there are larger economic problems. And the gap between the rich and the poor continues to widen, the rich needing the poor to keep whatever riches they have. And the ghetto dwellers grow desperate and begin to believe less and less that there is hope even for the next generation coming up. And crackheads crack heads and zip guns become uzis and gangs take on a corporate quality— Crips, Inc. and Bloods, Inc., national gang networks with corporate headquarters in Los Angeles. And their problems become everyone's problems in one sense or another. Economic problems, and the ways in which they shape our lives, hegemonically, place us all—Americans—in the same postmodern boat.

Concern over family, the loss of the community as a social entity, the need for two earners to have what had once been provided by one wage earner are not unique to this academic of color. Flex-time, split shifts, part-time are not matters of choice but matters of economic necessity, disallowing a cohesive, day-to-day family, a family that is necessarily small because one can ill afford the time, or the space, or the cost of the larger family. The academic or the classroom teacher may not punch clocks, but home hours are spent more on grading papers or performing research or publishing than tending to families. The clock punches us. Extended families are extended throughout the globe, as market forces, more than anything else, fling the various nuclei of what had once been the extended family hither and yon. Time for community is lost. Time in community is lost, again, as market forces have us moving from place to place. And we search for historical roots: oral histories or bumper stickers that read "Polish and proud of it."

> [A] sample study of North Chicago residents in 1977, finds, for example, that the objects actually valued in the home were not the "pecuniary trophies" of a materialist culture which acted as "religious indices of one's socio-economic class, age, gender, and so on," but the artifacts that embodied "ties to loved ones and kin, valued experiences and activities, and memories of significant life events and people." (Harvey 292)

There is a widespread search for longer-lasting values and more than economic security in a rapidly shifting world. All but a relative few are struggling for more time, more space, less motion.

The compression of space, time, and motion is the postmodern condition. And the ways we are kept in motion, working away time, vying for space, maintain fragmentation. The postmodern condition is writ large for the young, the elderly, the unemployed, the unemployable, the woman, the person of color. And each group does have historical, cultural, political, and economic conditions peculiar to that group. I can only really know and tell about one man of color's conditions. There are experiences that I no doubt have in common with others of color, experiences those not of color will never be a able to understand fully. By the same token, I can never know, not fully, the experiences of the white middle class. Yet we all have our commonalities. We are—all of us—affected by the hegemonic and by its fragmenting ideology of individualism. With every man for himself only a few will win out. We are individuals, but that doesn't mean we must dive headlong into

individualism. We need to cling to our various collectivities—Puerto
Rican, Latino, of color, academic, American—and they need not be
mutually exclusive if we consider them critically, and if we accept that
we carry contradictions. We all stand to gain by developing a critical
consciousness.

References

Abercrombie, Thomas J. "When the Moors Ruled Spain." *National Geographic* 174:1 (1988): 87–119.

Adamson, Walter L. *Hegemony and Revolution: A Study of Antonio Gramsci's Political and Cultural Theory.* Berkeley: U of California P, 1980.

Aiken, Susan Hardy. "Women and the Question of Canonicity." *College English* 48 (1986): 288–301.

Althusser, Louis. *For Marx.* New York: Vintage, 1969.

———. *Lenin and Philosophy and Other Essays.* Trans. Ben Brewster. New York: Monthly Review Press, 1971.

Anderson, Perry. *Considerations of Western Marxism.* 1976. London: Verso, 1979.

Aranowitz, Stanley, and Henry Giroux. *Education Under Siege: The Conservative, Liberal, and Radical Debate Over Schooling.* South Hadley, MA: Bergin and Garvey, 1985.

Arnott, Peter. *The Byzantines and Their World.* New York: St. Martin's, 1973.

Atkins, Chester G. "It can happen here." *EPIC Events: Newsletter of the English Plus Information Clearinghouse* 4 (1992): 1,4.

Barrera, Mario. *Race and Class in the Southwest: A Theory of Racial Inequality.* Notre Dame, IN: U of Notre Dame P, 1979.

Barthes, Roland. *Mythologies.* Trans. Annette Lavers. London: Hill and Wang, 1972.

Bartholomae, David, and Anthony Petrosky. *Facts, Artifacts, and Counterfacts: A Theory and Method for a Reading and Writing Course.* Upper Montclair, NJ: Boynton/Cook, 1986.

———. *Ways of Reading: An Anthology for Writers.* New York: St. Martin's, 1987.

Bergstrom, Robert F. "Discovery of Meaning: Development of Formal Thought in the Teaching of Literature." *College English* 45 (1983): 745–55.

Bernstein, Basil. *Class, Codes and Control: Towards a Theory of Educational Transmissions.* 3 vols. 2nd ed. Boston: Routledge & K. Paul, 1977.

Bizzell, Patricia. "Arguing about Literacy." *College English* 50 (1988): 141–53.

Boggs, Carl. *The Two Revolutions: Antonio Gramsci and the Dilemmas of Western Marxism.* Boston: South End, 1984.

Bonilla, Frank and Ricardo Campos. "A Wealth of Poor: Puerto Ricans in the New Economic Order." *Daedelus* (2): 134–76.

Browning, Robert. *The Byzantine Empire.* New York: Scribner, 1980.

Bruffee, Kenneth. "Collaborative Learning and the 'Conversation of Mankind.'" *College English* 46 (1984): 635–52.

———. Response. *College English* 49 (1987): 711–16.

Burke, Kenneth. *A Rhetoric of Motives.* Berkeley: U of California P, 1969.

Califa, Antonio J. "The attack on minority language speakers." Unpubl. paper. ACLU, Washington, D.C., 1 August 1991.

Cayer, R.L. and R.K. Sacks. "Oral and Written Discourse of Basic Writers: Similarities and Differences." *Research in the Teaching of English* 13 (1979): 121–28.

Chafe, Wallace. "Integration and Involvement in Speaking, Writing, and Oral Literature." In *Spoken and Written Language: Exploring Orality and Literacy.* Ed. Deborah Tannen. Norwood: Ablex. 35–53.

Christian Science Monitor. 27 Oct. 1988: 5.

Cirese, Alberta Maria. "Popular Culture: Gramsci's Observations on Folklore." In *Approaches to Gramsci.* Ed. Anne Showstack Sassoon. London: Writers and Readers, 1982.

Cohen, Arthur M. and Florence B. Brawer. *The American Community College.* 2nd ed. San Francisco: Jossey-Bass, 1989.

Conklin, Nancy Faires and Margaret A. Lourie. *A Host of Tongues: Language Communities in the United States.* New York: The Free Press, 1983.

Cooper, Charles R. and Lee Odell. "Considerations of Sound in the Composing Processes of Published Writers." *Research in the Teaching of English* 10 (1976): 103–15.

Crowley, Sharon. Personal communication.

D'Angelo, Frank. "Literacy and Cognition: A Developmental Perspective." In *Literacy for Life: The Demand for Reading and Writing.* Eds. R.W. Bailey and R.M. Fosheim. New York: Modern Language Association, 1983.

DeJesus, Carolina Maria. *Child of the Dark: The Diary of Carolina Maria deJesus.* Trans. David S. Clair. New York: E.P. Dutton, 1962.

Delpit, Lisa D. "The Silenced Dialogue: Power and Pedagogy in Educating Other People's Children." *Harvard Educational Review* 58 (1988): 280–98.

Dillon, George A. *Constructing Texts: Elements of a Theory of Composition and Style.* Bloomington: Indiana UP, 1981.

DuBois, W.E.B., *The Souls of Black Folk.* New York: New American Library, 1969.

Emecheta, Buchi. *Double Yoke.* New York: Braziller, 1982.

Emig, Janet. "Writing as a Mode of Learning." *College Composition and Communication* 28 (1977): 122–28.

English language amendment, 1984: Hearings on S.J. Res. 167 before the subcommittee on the Constitution of the Senate Judiciary Committee, 98th Cong., 2nd Sess. 1284 (1984). Washington, D.C.: Government Printing Office.

Entwistle, Harold. *Antonio Gramsci: Conservative Schooling for Radical Politics.* London: Routledge and K. Paul, 1979.

Estrada, Leobardo F., F. Chris García, Reynaldo Flores Macías, and Lionel Maldonado. "Chicanos in the United States: A History of Exploitation and Resistance." *Daedalus* Vol. 110, No. 2 (1981): 103–31.

Fagan, William T. "The Relationship of the 'Maze' to Language Planning and Production." *Research in the Teaching of English* 16 (1982): 85–95.

Fallows, J. "Bilingual education." *Crossing Cultures*. Eds. Henry Knepler and Myrna Knepler. New York: Macmillan, 1987. 378–88.

Farrell, Thomas J. "IQ and Standard English." *College Composition and Communication* 34 (1983): 470–84.

Femia, Joseph V. *Gramsci's Political Thought: Hegemony, Consciousness, and the Revolutionary Process*. Oxford: Clarendon, 1981.

Flores, Juan, John Attinasi, and Pedro Pedraza, Jr. "*La Carreta Made a U-Turn:* Puerto Rican Language and Culture in the United States." *Daedalus* Vol. 110, No. 2 (1981): 193–217.

Flower, Linda. "Cognition, Context, and Theory Building." *College Composition and Communication* 40 (1989): 282–311.

Fordham, Signithia. "Racelessness as a Factor in Black Students' School Success: Pragmatic Strategy or Pyrrhic Victory? *Harvard Education Review* 58 (1988): 54–84.

Franklin, John Hope. "The Land of Room Enough." *Daedalus* 110 (1981): 1–12.

Freire, Paulo. *Cultural Action for Freedom*. Cambridge, MA: *Harvard Educational Review* and Center for the Study of Development and Social Change, 1970.

———. *Pedagogy of the Oppressed*. Trans. Myra Bergman Ramos. New York: Herder and Herder, 1970.

Freire, Paulo and Donaldo Macedo. *Literacy: Reading the Word and the World*. South Hadley, MA: Bergin and Garvey, 1987.

Galarza, Ernesto. *Barrio Boy*. Notre Dame, IN: U of Notre Dame P, 1971.

Galbraith, John Kenneth. *The Culture of Contentment*. New York: Houghton Mifflin. 1992.

Gilyard, Keith. *Voices of the Self: A Study of Language Competence*. Detroit: Wayne State UP, 1991.

Giroux, Henry. *Theory and Resistance in Education: A Pedagogy for the Opposition*. London: Heinemann, 1983.

Grabe, William and Robert Kaplan. "Writing in a Second Language: Contrastive Rhetoric." In *Richness in Writing: Empowering ESL Students*. Eds. Donald M. Johnson and Duane H. Roen. New York: Longman, 1989. 263–83.

Gramsci, Antonio. *Selections from the Prison Notebooks*. Ed. and Trans. Quiten Hoare and Geoffrey Nowell-Smith. New York: International, 1971.

———. *Selections from Cultural Writings*. Ed. David Forgacs and Geoffrey Nowell-Smith. Trans. William Boelhower. Cambridge: Harvard UP, 1985.

Hairston, Maxine. "Diversity, Ideology, and Teaching Writing."*College Composition and Communication* 43 (1992): 179–93.

Hakuta, K. Public testimony to the Connecticut State Legislature. 30 March 1987.

Hartwell, Patrick. "Dialect Interference in Writing: A Critical View." *Research in the Teaching of English* 14 (1980): 101–18.

Harvey, David. *The Condition of Postmodernity: An Enquiry into the Origins of Cultural Change*. Cambridge, MA: Blackwell, 1990.

Haswell, Richard H. "Minimal Marking." *College English* 45 (1983): 600–604.

Hayakawa, S.I. "Why English should be our official language." *The Educational Digest*. May 1987: 36–37.

———. "Why the English Language Amendment?" *English Journal* 76: (1987): 14–16.

Heath, Shirley Brice. "A National Language Academy?: Debate in the New Nation." *International Journal of the Sociology of Language* 11 (1976): 9–43.

———. "Protean Shapes in Literacy Events: Ever-Shifting Oral and Literate Tendencies." In *Spoken and Written Language*. Ed. Deborah Tannen. Norwood, NJ: Ablex, 1982. 91–117.

———. *Ways with Words: Language, Life, and Work in Communities and Classrooms*. New York: Cambridge UP, 1983.

Hirsch, E.D., Jr. *Cultural Literacy: What Every American Needs to Know*. Boston: Houghton Mifflin, 1987.

———. *The Philosophy of Composition*. Chicago: U of Chicago P, 1977.

Jameson, Fredric. *Marxism and Form: Twentieth-Century Dialectical Theories of Literature*. Princeton: Princeton UP, 1971.

Jenkins, Romilly. *Byzantium: The Imperial Centuries, AD 610–1071*. Toronto: U of Toronto P, 1966.

Jensen, Arthur R. "The Differences Are Real." *Psychology Today* 7 (1973): 80–82, 84, 86.

———. "How Much Can We Boost IQ and Scholastic Achievement?" *Harvard Education Review* 39 (1969): 1–123.

Johnson, Michael L. "Hell is the Place We Don't Know We're In: The Control-Dictions of Cultural Literacy, Strong Reading, and Poetry." *College English* 50 (1988): 309–317.

Kaplan, Robert B. "Cultural Thought Patterns and Intercultural Education." *Language Learning* 16 (1966): 1–20.

Kennedy, George. *Classical Rhetoric and Its Christian and Secular Tradition from Ancient to Modern Times*. Chapel Hill: U of North Carolina P, 1980.

Labov, William. "Academic Ignorance and Black Intelligence." *Atlantic Monthly* 229:6 (1972): 59–68.

———. *Language in the Inner City: Studies in the Black English Vernacular*. Philadelphia: U of Pennsylvania P, 1972.

Lefebvre, Henri. "Toward a Leftist Cultural Politics: Remarks Occasioned by the Centenary of Marx's Death." Trans. David Reifman. In *Marxism and the Interpretation of Culture*. Eds. Cary Nelson and Lawrence Grossberg. Urbana: U of Illinois P, 1988.

LeFevre, Karen Burke. *Invention as a Social Act*. Carbondale: Southern Illinois UP, 1987.

Leff, Michael C. "In Search of Ariadne's Thread: A Review of the Recent Literature on Rhetorical Theory." *Central States Speech Journal* 29 (1978): 73–91.

LeFranchia, H. "Election '88: The mountain west." *The Christian Science Monitor.* 28 October 1988: 18.

Lenin, V.I. *What is to be Done? Burning Questions of Our Movement.* New York: International, 1969.

Liem, Nguyen Dang. "Bilingual-Bicultural Education for Indochinese." Symposium for Asian and Pacific American Education: Direction in the 1980's. San Francisco, 25–27 April 1979.

———. "English as a Second Language for Indochinese." Annual TESOL Convention. San Francisco, 3–9 March 1980.

Lunsford, Andrea. "Cognitive Development and the Basic Writer." *College English* 41 (1979): 38–46.

Lux, Paul and William Grabe. "Multivariate Approaches to Contrastive Rhetoric." *Linguas Modernas* 18 (1991): 133–160.

Markels, Robin Bell. *A New Perspective on Cohesion in Expository Paragraphs.* Carbondale: Southern Illinois UP, 1984.

Marx, Karl. "On the Jewish Question." *The Marx-Engels Reader.* Ed. Robert C. Tucker. 2nd ed. New York: Norton, 1978.

McCoonnell, James V. "Confessions of a Scientific Humorist." *Impact* 19 (1969): 3–9.

McQuade, Donald. "Living In—And On—the Margins." *College Composition and Communication* 43 (1992): 11–22.

Montaño-Harmon, María Rosario. "Discourse Features of Written Mexican Spanish: Current Research in Contrastive Rhetoric and Its Implications." *Hispania* 74 (1991): 417–25.

Murguía, Edward. *Assimilation, Colonialism, and the Mexican American People.* Austin: Center for Mexican American Studies, 1975.

Murray, Donald M. "All Writing is Autobiography." *College Composition and Communication* 42 (1991): 66–74.

———. "Internal Revision: A Process of Discovery." In *Research on Composing: Points of Departure.* Eds. Charles R. Cooper and Lee Odell. Urbana, IL: NCTE, 1978.

Myers, Greg. "Reality, Consensus, and Reform in the Rhetoric of Composition Teaching." *College English* 48 (1986): 154–74.

Nelson, Cary and Lawrence Grossberg (eds.). *Marxism and the Interpretation of Culture.* Urbana, IL: U of Illinois P, 1988.

Ogbu, John U. *Minority Education and Caste: The American System in Cross-Cultural Perspective.* New York: Academic, 1978.

Ohmann, Richard. "Graduate Students, Professionals, Intellectuals." *College English* 52 (1990): 247–57.

———. *Politics of Letters.* Middleton: Wesleyan UP, 1987.

Ostler, Shirley E. "English in Parallels: A Comparison of English and Arabic Prose." In *Writing Across Languages: Analysis of L2 Text.* Eds. Ulla Connor and Robert B. Kaplan. Reading, MA: Addison-Wesley, 1987.

Perl, Sondra. "The Composing Processes of Unskilled College Writers." *Research in the Teaching of English* 13 (1979): 317–36.

Reyes, María de la Luz, and John J. Halcón, "Racism in Academia: The Old Wolf Revisited." *Harvard Education Review* 58 (1988): 299–314.

Rodriguez, Richard. *Hunger of Memory: The Education of Richard Rodriguez.* New York: Bantam, 1982.

Rose, Mike. *Lives on the Boundary: The Struggles of America's Underprepared.* New York: Free Press, 1988.

———. "Narrowing the Mind and Page: Remedial Writers and Cognitive Reductionism." *College Composition and Communication* 39 (1988): 267–302.

Santana-Seda, Sister Olga. *A Contrastive Study in Rhetoric: An Analysis of the Organization of English and Spanish Paragraphs Written by Native Speakers of Each Language.* Diss. New York U, 1974.

Sassoon, Anne Showstack, ed. *Approaches to Gramsci.* London: Writers and Readers, 1982.

Scholes, Robert. Review: "Three Views of Education: Nostalgia, History, and Voodoo." *College English* 50 (1988): 323–32.

Schuster, Charles I. "Mikhail Bakhtin as Rhetorical Theorist." *College English* 47 (1985): 594–607.

Scribner, Sylvia and Michael Cole. *The Psychology of Literacy.* Cambridge, MA: Harvard UP, 1981.

Shahid, Irfan. *Byzantium and the Arabs in the Fifth Century.* Washington, DC: Dumbarton Oaks, 1989.

Shor, Ira and Paulo Freire. *A Pedagogy for Liberation: Dialogues on Transforming Education.* South Hadley, MA: Bergin & Harvey, 1987.

Silko, Leslie Marmon. *Ceremony.* New York: Penguin. 1986.

Sommers, Nancy. "Responding to Student Writing." *College Composition and Communication* 33 (1982): 148–56.

Spellmeyer, Kurt. "Foucault and the Freshman Writer: Considering the Self in Discourse." *College English* 51 (1989): 715–29.

Stavrianos, Lev S. *Global Rift: The Third World Comes of Age.* New York: Morrow, 1981.

Superintendent of Public Instruction. *Minority Enrollments in Public and Private Schools: State of Washington.* Olympia: SPI, 1983.

Tannen, Deborah. "The Oral/Literate Continuum in Discourse." In *Spoken and Written Language: Explaining Orality and Literacy.* Ed. D. Tannen. Norwood: Ablex, 1982. 1–16.

Trimbur, John. "Consensus and Difference in Collaborative Learning." *College English* 51 (1989): 602–16.

Vachek, Josef. *Written Language: General Problems and Problems of English.* The Hague: Mouton, 1973.

West, Cornel. "Marxist Theory and the Specificity of Afro-American Oppression." *Marxism and the Interpretation of Culture.* Eds. Cary Nelson and Lawrence Grossberg. Urbana: U of Illinois P, 1988.

———. "Minority Discourse and the Pitfalls of Canon Formation." *Yale Journal of Criticism* 1:1 (1987): 193–201.

Wilkie, Richard W. "Karl Marx on Rhetoric." *Philosophy and Rhetoric* 9 (1976): 232–46.

Wingert, P. "Say it in English." *Newsweek.* 20 Feb 1989: 22–23.

Witte, Stephen P. and Lester Faigley. "Coherence, Cohesion, and Writing Quality." *College Composition and Communication* 32 (1981): 189–204.

Wright, Erik Olin. *Classes.* London: Verso, 1985.

Zentella, Ana Celia. "The Language Situation of Puerto Ricans." *Language Diversity: Problem or Resource?* Eds. Sandra Lee McKay and Sau-ling Cynthia Wong. Cambridge, MA: Newbury, 1988. 140–65.

Author

Victor Villanueva, Jr., an associate professor at Northern Arizona University who teaches writing and rhetoric there, and who studies and writes about the politics of rhetoric and its effects on people of color, describes himself as "a husband, a parent, a professor, and a happy man."